Tactical Entanglements

Martin Zeilinger (Senior Lecturer in Computational Art and Technology, Abertay University) is an Austrian researcher and curator currently based in Dundee, Scotland. His work focuses on critical artistic approaches to emerging blockchain and AI technologies, intellectual property issues in contemporary art, and aspects of experimental videogame culture. He has co-curated Vector Festival (Toronto) since 2014, and organized the 2019 MoneyLab symposium (London). His research is available in books such as *Artists Re:Thinking the Blockchain* and the *MoneyLab Reader 2*, and journals including *Philosophy & Technology*, *Culture Machine*, and *Media Theory*.
// marjz.net / @mrtnzlngr

Tactical Entanglements: AI Art, Creative Agency, and the Limits of Intellectual Property

Martin Zeilinger

μ meson press

Financial support for this publication was provided through the Abertay University Open Access Publication Fund.

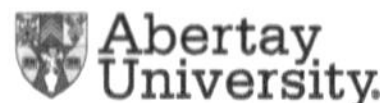

The cover shows an AI-generated image output created by the AI artist and researcher Tom White (https://drib.net/). Reminiscent of the now-famous AI artwork *Portrait of Edmond Belamy* and the authorship dispute it sparked (discussed in chapter 4), the images "were made by [White] using [Robbie Barrat's] code to show that [Obvious Collective] could have done the same" (Artnome 2018).

Bibliographical Information of the German National Library
The German National Library lists this publication in the Deutsche Nationalbibliografie (German National Bibliography); detailed bibliographic information is available online at http://dnb.d-nb.de.

Published in 2021 by meson press, Lüneburg, Germany
www.meson.press

Design concept: Torsten Köchlin, Silke Krieg
Copy editing: Isobel Campbell

The print edition of this book is printed by Lightning Source, Milton Keynes, United Kingdom.

ISBN (Print): 978-3-95796-183-9
ISBN (PDF): 978-3-95796-184-6
ISBN (EPUB): 978-3-95796-185-3
DOI: 10.14619/1839

The digital edition of this publication can be downloaded freely at: www.meson.press.

Contents

Acknowledgements

Book-writing is an amazingly collaborative effort, considering how alienating and lonely it can feel. In the pandemic-stricken year of social isolation during which I wrote most of this book, my work has occasioned very stimulating conversations and discussions with friends, colleagues, artists, and academic peers around the world, for which I'm immensely grateful. Thank you to friends and colleagues old and new, near and far, many of whom offered to look at and think about parts of the manuscript in its various iterations, and who provided feedback, encouragement, words of warning, questions, answers, or other kindnesses. They include Danilo Mandic, Tina Kendall, Ronald Ng, Andrew Bricker, Greg Smith, Bruce Lai and Katrina Lagacé, Jason Bailey at Artnome, Jeff Thompson, Nicky Hamlyn, Patricia de Vries, as well as Christos Michalakos, Hadi Mehrpouya, Joseph De Lappe, Darshana Jayemanne, and Drew Hemment in and around Dundee.

My critical perspective has been shaped in important ways by conversations with several of the artists whose work I discuss in the book—particularly Maja Smrekar, Adam Basanta, and Jake Elwes. Thank you for sharing your work and insights so generously.

The book in its final form also gained tremendously from insightful commentary and critical remarks on a first draft, received from my excellent reviewers Carys Craig and Andreas Broeckmann.

I am very grateful for the supportive welcome I received at Abertay University's School of Design and Informatics, where I took up employment around the time I began working on the book. In particular, thank you to Dr. Dayna Galloway (Head of the Division of Games and Art), Professor Gregor White (Dean of School), and Professor Nia White (Dean of Graduate School) for supporting this publication through the university's Open Access Fund. Thanks also to Andreas Kirchner and everyone at meson press, for taking on the project at a difficult time, and for seeing it through so efficiently.

To many other friends, thanks for your patience in dealing with cancelled bike rides, skipped movie nights, postponed visits, unanswered phone calls, and much-delayed email replies—I have much yet to learn about book-life balance.

Lastly, the biggest thanks goes to my family, for your enduring support, and to Deniz Johns, for all your love, encouragement, wisdom and understanding.

[1]

Introduction: From Agency to Property, from AI to IP

This book explores digital artists' experiments with emerging technologies of artificial intelligence (AI) in order to formulate a critique of how AI is impacting and reshaping the concepts of agency and ownership. The concerns underlying this focus can be roughly summarized as follows: on the one hand, AI appears to gesture toward new paradigms of thinking, acting and being that promise a push beyond ideological horizons centered on the human(ist) agent; but on the other hand, AI is deeply entangled with socio-economic and political regimes that rely on precisely this subject position, often in problematic alignments with the capitalist logic of contemporary ownership models. AI, in this sense, exists in a diffuse border region between the compelling idea of emerging non-human agency (embodied in the very notion of 'artificial intelligence' itself) and the all-too human contexts in which contemporary AI tends to manifest (for example as algorithmic control mechanisms in the domains of work, governance, law, finance, or entertainment). Using AI art as my core subject of analysis and discussion, I want to consider what interventions can be staged in anthropocentric ownership models by rethinking agency in and through AI. I will argue that critical uses of AI in digital art can be ideally suited for disturbing conventional notions of the singular, unified artist figure, of the unique artwork, and of anthropocentric perspectives on creativity as such. AI art can thus speculate on critical reconfigurations of creative agency—and therefore also on the potential destabilization of intellectual property (IP) models that continue to rely on the integrity the human(ist) agent as creator and owner.

My discussion is not going to echo spectacularizing assertions that AI is "becoming creative" in the sense of fully autonomous computational entities capable of matching and exceeding the aesthetic, artistic, and artful expressions of humans. In my view, claims of emergent AI creativity tend to be marred by problematic anthropocentric biases, both regarding the concepts of creativity perpetuated in such claims, and regarding the humanistic ownership models underpinned by these concepts of creativity. Rather than trying to imagine an AI art in which human artists are supplanted by human-like creative machines, I want to explore what collaborative entanglements exist between artists and AI, and consider the critical ends toward which such entanglements can be oriented. What new types of artistic practice, what reconfigurations of the author function, what new forms of creative and critical expression can be seen to manifest, in what I will call the works and workings of posthumanist agential assemblages?

Given my focus on agency and ownership, two domains of critical thought are particularly important for this discussion. The first is law, and more specifically theories of intellectual property, which form a key critical interface between art, expressive agency, and the cultural and socio-economic environments within which they are embedded. The second is posthumanist thought, which I consider to be among the most useful frameworks for exploring the critical valences of AI in digital art. The conjunction of legal theory and posthumanism allows me to foreground discrepancies and productive contradictions between the two frameworks when it comes to issues of creative expression, agency, and ownership.

Throughout, I draw on posthumanism in a sense similar to that in which Gary Hall has described it, namely as a perspective that "is concerned with the displacement of the unified, self-reflexive, and rational humanist subject from its central place in the world as a result of the erosion of the human's 'natural' boundaries with the animal, technology, and the environment" (Hall 2016, 93). In the context of AI art projects that recalibrate the shape and meaning of creative agency, such a perspective facilitates a departure from the "traditional liberal humanist model that comes replete with clichéd, ready-made . . . ideas of proprietorial authorship, . . . originality, fixity, and the finished object" (xiv).

A discussion of legal technicalities concerning copyright and authorship might seem at a considerable remove from key concerns of AI art as such. But it must be kept in mind that a key effect of IP law is its codification of broadly accepted notions concerning the nature of creative expression and authorship—notions that AI art frequently addresses quite directly. Practically speaking, IP laws are formulated with the aim of being inclusive and adaptive. Nevertheless, the law outlines prescriptive requirements regarding what an artwork can be, who (or what) its author can be, how a specific artwork can circulate, and how this circulation can be controlled. If IP law is understood as a key manifestation of broadly accepted views on and attitudes toward authorship and cultural ownership, then there is certainly much to discuss in relation to AI art projects that problematize or disturb views and attitudes codified in the law. Such discussion has particular critical purchase in a number of contexts addressed in later chapters: for example where the algorithmic enforcement of copyright law is concerned, and where proprietary and black-boxed algorithmic systems are used to implement complex legal norms and standards; or also where AI art implements tactics aimed at challenging the integrity of the ownership models that are expressed in IP law, in technology uses sanctioned by the law, and in humanist views on authorship and creative expression underlying the law's prescriptions.

Building on Christiane Paul's widely adopted definition of digital art (2016), I define AI art, most generally, as digital art that incorporates technologies of artificial intelligence as a medium. By this I mean that AI art utilizes AI, and that it implements AI practically even when it does not engage AI thematically. AI art, in other words, is not necessarily about AI. Other cultural theorists of AI have calibrated their focus quite differently: Joanna Zylinska, for example, proposes that "one of the most creative—and most needed—ways in which artists can use AI is *by telling better stories about AI*" (2020, 31; emphasis in original). In the context of my own discussion, I would agree that every AI artist (by which I mean every human artist working with AI) must speculate on the existence and potentialities of non-human creative agency. But I would also emphasize that there can be important differences between narrativizing such speculation and developing it in a mode of practical experimentation. In my opinion, one such difference is that in the many fabulations of AI art, crucial details concerning the functionality or outputs of AI systems can be easily glossed over, simplified, or obfuscated (one example of this kind of rhetorical blackboxing of AI is addressed in my discussion of *Portrait of Edmond Belamy* in chapter 4). My main focus is therefore on AI art projects in which critical speculation is enacted structurally, based on a practical engagement with AI technologies. In the AI art projects discussed in the following chapters, this will be seen to manifest in a kind of hacking of AI that interrogates AI's own abilities to hack concepts including those of agency, creativity, and ownership.

True to AI's origins in the military-industrial complex, and true to the support its development now receives from corporate tech giants, mainstream implementations of AI tend to perpetuate and amplify very narrow perspectives on agency and ownership. This occurs in alignment with ideological frameworks that have been variously described, for example, as computational capitalism (Stiegler 2019), cognitive capitalism (Boutang 2011), communicative capitalism (Dean 2005), or surveillance capitalism

(Zuboff 2019). Mainstream AI, in other words, tends to serve socio-economic regimes that rely on the automation, high-speed calculation, data-intensive analysis, predictive techniques, and communicative abilities that computation affords. As a result, AI applications can constitute frightful surveillance tools, restrictive digital rights management systems, manipulative recommendation algorithms, biased personal assistants, Kafkaesque algorithmic governance frameworks, or exploitative high-speed stock trading protocols. Based on these and other sinister realities of contemporary AI, Nick Dyer-Witheford, Atle M. Kjosen and James Steinhoff (2019) put forward the dark notion that the inhuman power of AI may end up emancipating capital from humanity, rather than the other way around. What I want to argue is that AI also offers important opportunities for practice-based experimentation that can recast the ideological imbrications of the underlying technologies very differently. This, perhaps, is the speculative core of my argument in this book: diverging from Nick Land's notion of AI as a fundamentally capitalist technology (Land 2012), I want to explore how, in cultural contexts, AI might also be framed as a tactical anti-capitalist tool, at least in the sense that it is capable of producing and enacting new perspectives on creative practice, authorship, and the artwork that challenge prevailing notions of human(ist) creative agency, and the cultural logic of intellectual property derived from it.

Today, the field of AI art can appear as a creative industries "sector" that is defined, driven and dominated by corporate funders. This impression is conveyed, for example, by the many AI art residencies and project grants sponsored by Google, Amazon, Facebook, Microsoft, and other corporate entities described by Bernard Stiegler as the "new barbarians" that are closing off horizons of technology-based possibility, in efforts to foreclose our ability to expand or reconfigure such horizons (2019). But the digital art communities within which AI art flourishes have also been crucially shaped by open source culture, radical philosophies of open access to knowledge and technology, by the activist approaches of tactical media, the hacker ethics of the early internet, and the ideals of a cultural commons. It is against this background that I want to develop my discussion of AI art projects which problematize the humanist vision of the singular, unified human agent; of the spirited (genius?) individual as sole originator of creative expressions; of the human as self-interested proprietor of the fruits of their labor; and of aesthetic, legal, and socio-economic paradigms that model restrictive property regimes around this kind of agent. In adopting a post-humanist perspective, my emphasis is instead on the potential for AI art to instantiate agency as relational, decentered and plural, and to approach creative practice as fundamentally dynamic and embedded.

In what follows, current AI art projects (most of them under-taken since 2018, or still in development at the time of writing) serve as the scaffolding for a broader discussion that spans overlapping discursive fields to integrate posthumanism and law with aesthetics, media theory, and political economy. Across all of these domains, the concepts of agency and ownership are key to understanding how human subjects have been idealized as presumptively free, self-determining, and self-owning; how this idealization feeds into still-prevailing definitions of creative expression, authorship, and the artwork itself; and how these definitions have helped to rationalize a framing of the artist as a quasi-neoliberalist free agent whose activities and desires align with predominant ownership models. Against this backdrop, how are agency and ownership inflected when artificial intelligence comes into the picture?

Mainstream AI development certainly contradicts the utopian tone of predictions that AI will be (or already is) capable of intelligent behavior, that it may soon display traits of agency previously reserved for natural persons, and that it is in the process of becoming creative. It points, instead, in the direction of AI-driven surveillance capitalism, corporate control over networked communication systems, and the rampant financialization of everyday (digital) life. In these contexts, the centrality of the human agent persists, even if only in the interpellation of disembodied data subjects that continue to produce and consume, to own and owe in alignment with exploitative capitalist ideologies. In cultural contexts, likewise, the humanist, anthropocentric notion of the singular, unified artist figure persists, and even where digital culture courts ideals of sharing, free access, or easy reproducibility, much of it is nevertheless structured by a property-oriented fencing-in of individual creative agency. Overall, a key linchpin around which digital culture and digital art continue to turn is the cultural logic of intellectual property. A key question pursued in what follows is how this logic may be challenged when AI art pushes for a rethinking of agency beyond the centrality and supremacy of the human(ist) subject as author and proprietor, and when it reorients itself toward emergent forms of posthumanist agential assemblages that contradict existing property paradigms. As I will argue, in such configurations expressive agency is located beyond the confines of the human artist, and co-exists with them in productive, intra-actional entanglements that integrate *anthropos* with computer hardware, software, algorithms, and other tools, crafts, or knowledge on which the artist relies. As will be seen, this discussion does not abandon the humanist subject entirely, but rather recalibrates it in relation to the ecologies in which it shares.

Agency is most generally understood as the manifestation of a capacity to act. But the concept is also intimately tied to questions of self-determination, autonomy, expressive freedom, and the ability to own property. How, then, is agency constituted in the age of AI? Who or what is an agent now? What new aesthetic, legal, and socio-economic contours and limits of agency emerge in AI? How does human agency relate to its algorithmic and machinic others? What new horizons of critique become possible when creative agency, in its links to authorship and ownership, are rethought in and through AI, in speculative approximations of posthumanist agential assemblages whose works and workings push beyond anthropocentric and humanist ontologies of creativity and artfulness, intellectual property and cultural ownership?

Decentering Human Agency in AI Art

Let me offer two introductory examples that resonate with many of these questions. The first focuses on the work of the British artist Anna Ridler, who frequently uses machine learning (ML) to explore issues of creativity, authorship, and ownership. Among Ridler's key strategies for doing so is the use of custom, artist-assembled datasets. The artist has described this as a powerful political act that can help move past the exclusionary tendencies ingrained in mainstream AI (Ridler 2020). This approach is well exemplified in *Mosaic Virus* (2019), a three-channel video installation that depicts morphing formations of AI-generated images of tulips (fig. 1). The work focuses on the historical "tulip mania" phenomenon and explores enduring human obsessions with agency and ownership through the themes of monetary wealth and financial speculation. The tulip mania phenomenon dates to 1630s Holland, when tulips had become highly sought-after flowers, and certain tulip bulbs were seen as items of immense value. The perceived value of the bulbs was linked to rare color stripes caused by a plant virus, which would—unpredictably—appear on some tulip petals. At the time, the behavior of the so-called mosaic virus was poorly understood, and botanists were unable to control how it propagated the prized petal stripes. This led to frantic trading in tulip bulbs, and what is now considered one of the first speculative financial bubbles. In Ridler's installation, the unpredictable effects of the virus and its destabilizing effect on the value of tulip bulbs allegorize the speculative desires that both art and finance can inspire. Specifically, *Mosaic Virus* links the instability of values bound in commodified artefacts to the perceived unknowability of the computational technologies used in creating the work. The work thus thematizes a decentering of human agency, its redistribution across non-human systems, and the impact of this redistribution on questions of monetary value and ownership.

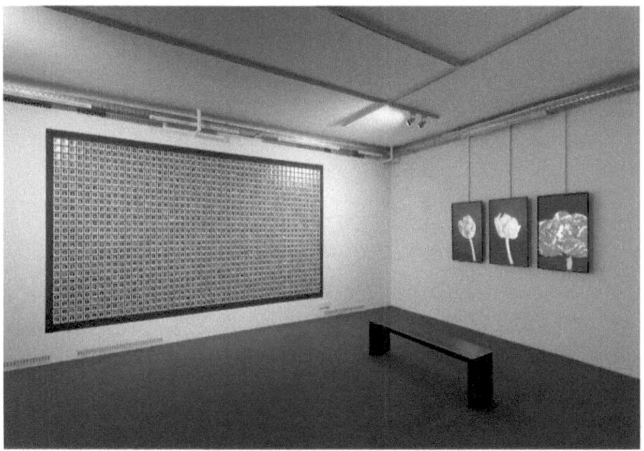

[Figure 1] Anna Ridler, installation view of "The Abstraction of Nature," solo exhibition at Aksioma, Ljubljana (2020). Photo credit: Domen Pal / Aksioma.

The use of a generative AI system is key to how this is conveyed to the viewer, because it extends questions of monetary value and ownership to the aesthetic realm and the concept of authorial control. To create *Mosaic Virus*, Ridler used a Generative Adversarial Network (GAN), a type of machine learning technology capable of generating novel outputs on the basis of large datasets of pre-existing material. (In-depth discussion of GAN-style generative image synthesis is offered in chapter 4, and also in Zeilinger 2021). The system was trained to generate ever-changing images of (inexistent) tulips using an artist-created dataset of roughly 10,000 hand-labelled photographs of actual tulips, and the outputs were additionally inflected by the ever-changing value of Bitcoin tokens (a speculative object of desire *par excellence*). Because the project uses a training dataset painstakingly assembled by the artist, *Mosaic Virus* conveys a strong sense that the artist retains a high level of creative agency (fig. 1 shows parts of the dataset exhibited alongside the video installation). The operational logic of GAN systems, however, lends the outputs a level of unpredictability, which is further amplified by the well-known volatility of Bitcoin token value. As a result, just as it may be impossible to authoritatively predict the value of tulip bulbs affected by a virus, so it becomes difficult to precisely locate creative agency in an artwork produced by a posthumanist agential assemblage of human artist, generative AI system, and erratic cryptocurrency valuation data.

Given the focus of this book, the nature of Ridler's training dataset strikes me as a particularly important parameter in the conceptual equation of *Mosaic Virus*: it foregrounds the presence of the artist in the creative process, while also highlighting the limited agency Ridler has in controlling outputs of the AI system she designed. The chosen medium and thematic framing offer a good context for a self-reflexive exploration of the limits of agency: the triad of generative AI, cryptocurrency, and plant virus can serve as a fitting "blackbox" of unpredictability into which anxieties concerning the limits of human control (i.e., the control of both authors and owners) can be projected. Based on this reading, I see as a central critical aim of *Mosaic Virus* its reflection on emerging digitally-bound value systems in which speculative fantasies of power and wealth become linked to questions of authorship, ownership, and agency. Here, non-human spaces of presumptive unknowability—the viral, the algorithmic—run up against all-too human obsessions with monetary and aesthetic value and authorial control. In other words, faced with complex non-human systems such as viruses, AI, or the blockchain, anthropocentric fantasies of control can dissolve into wild speculation, and the centrality of human agency is recalibrated in much more complex distributions across posthumanist assemblages.

Importantly, this reading is also somewhat undermined by Ridler's own suggestion that human agency—enacted in the significant degree of control the artist exerts over the training data—remains central to artistic uses of AI (2020). The artist's process of hand-assembling datasets is incredibly onerous; it rightfully presents itself as craft, as an artful process through which human intervention in the workings of AI is rendered as a valuable creative act. Ultimately, this provokes an interesting contradiction, since the project mobilizes the perceived unpredictability of generative AI outputs as a playful challenge to the very assumption of human mastery.

A different example indicates that the theme of agency is also a powerful lure for AI artists who are less concerned with critical interrogations of the concept. *Contrapposto* (2020), an AI-generated sculptural work by the American artist Ben Snell, struggles to locate new forms of non-human agency and creative expression meaningfully in AI. The amorphous sculpture, visually reminiscent of Henry Moore bronzes, is part of the artist's *Inheritance* series, which is "inspired by the classics" (presumably a nod to images of canonical sculptural work that constitute the training data) and "made from the pulverized computer that dreamt it" (Snell 2020; an image of the work is available to view on the referenced website). The sculpture thus consists of "flecks of silicon, copper, aluminum, plastic and pcb [...]. Within these bits exist the memories, the thoughts and thought-making power of the machine which created it. Its existence comes full circle in this new form, embodied with a newfound aura and agency" (ibid.). This framing is both intriguing and confusing. The artist clearly wishes to attribute creative agency to the computational system used in creating the work; formally, however, absolute dominion over this same system is asserted. Given the material form of the sculpture and the method of how it was made, it is unclear how or where agency is supposed to be situated here. Is it centered around a particular entity (the machine, the algorithm, the artwork), or is it distributed across dissolving boundaries between them? Does it open up a new horizon of creativity (AI as a speculative signifier of emerging posthumanist subjectivity), or doesn't it, rather, demarcate a limit (AI as a pseudo-autonomous tool used by a human artist)?

Contrapposto anthropomorphizes AI in the strongest terms. Visually, it invokes the master sculptors of the art history canon, and the series title positions the work as the literal offspring of these traditions. All around, the work is clearly meant to gesture toward a new kind of creativity embodied in computational technology, which is described as being "reborn" in the sculpture, where its processing powers "live on" (Snell n.d.). But it is precisely through this anthropocentric framing that the work ultimately reverts to the domineering centrality of the humanist artist figure who, after all, has "ground the computers to dust" (ibid.) in creating the sculpture (see Vincent 2019 for images of this process). This makes it difficult not to read *Contrapposto* as stillborn (to stay with the anthropocentric jargon). If some new kind of non-human creative agency was indeed present in this work, then the artist's production of the sculpture signals its extermination and embalming. The work, in this sense, undermines its own claims regarding the existence of non-human expressive agency, which is here immediately objectified in a clearly human-made, unique, commercially traded aesthetic artefact. Through this contradiction, the work nevertheless resonates with the conceptual rubric that organizes this book, and the sculpture offers a useful staging area for some of the central concerns I want to unpack in what follows. Where is the line between the anthropomorphized AI-system-as-artist and other, more radical new kinds of non-human expressive agency? How can digital art practices that draw on AI push beyond merely instrumentalizing the technology for the perpetuation of existing, anthropocentric views on authorship in new contexts?

What my brief discussion of *Mosaic Virus* and *Contrapposto* has not touched on so far is the problem of explicitly locating "authorship" across aesthetic, socio-economic, and legal contexts. I expect that most (human) audiences would approach the two foregoing examples as aesthetic artefacts that were clearly created by humans. Does this mean that their invocation of non-human agency is merely a rhetorical conceit, a story that is being told about AI? In the following chapters, I will locate a key critical potential of AI in its ability to highlight and foreground generative processes that structurally undermine conventional assumptions concerning the integrity and centrality of human creative agency and authorship. Again, such an undermining does not necessarily imply that AI systems can become authors or artists. But it certainly helps with clarifying the contradictions inherent in claims of AI creativity that are themselves modelled on anthropocentric, humanist frameworks of authorship. Such issues become particularly interesting in the context of competing (human) ownership claims linked to AI-generated artworks, and in legal disputes in which human artists may wish to deny their own creative agency by designating AI systems as authors.

AI and Creativity in the Intellectual Property Milieu

To rethink authorship in AI contexts inevitably requires a reassessment of key assumptions concerning the nature of creative expression. To my mind, influence, imitation, copying, and reusing are at the core of all artistic practice and (human) creativity. The lines between mimicry and mimesis are blurry, and the most fascinating works of art often emerge out of approaches that entail appropriation, repetition, or iteration. Such approaches are well established and highly visible in everything from digital remix culture and audio sampling to appropriation art and the collage arts of the earlier 20th century. Appropriation-based artistic techniques in particular have always had a tendency to provoke much controversy because they challenge the socio-economic logic of authorship-*qua*-ownership, as well as the humanist ideals based on which intellectual property itself is conceptualized. This includes IP's emphasis on originality and uniqueness as imprints of aesthetic and economic value, as well as its tight restrictions over how the knowledge and value bound in creative expressions can circulate. Where art transgresses narrowly conceived ideals of cultural ownership, IP law is quick to step in. Copyright, with its emphasis on originality and exclusive authorship rights, is a prime example of the conceptual flattening that occurs when creativity, in my view a profoundly dynamic and relational phenomenon, is reshaped to fit property-oriented paradigms that position the individualized human agent (or its corporate proxies) as the "natural" owner of creative expressions.

The digital is at strong odds with such paradigms for many reasons, not least because of how fundamentally (and obviously) digital technologies rely on processes of copying and reusing. Notably, such processes also figure importantly in many of the generative behaviors that characterize AI, including the underlying "training" and "learning" techniques. I will argue, therefore, that in AI contexts the issues outlined here can be significantly amplified. As I will discuss in a later chapter, legal theory is beginning to consider, for example, whether the assembling and use of training datasets constitutes large-scale IP rights infringement similar to the unauthorized publication of copyrighted texts—even when the data in question remains blackboxed within AI systems and never takes "human-readable" forms. All of this becomes even more complicated (and more interesting) when AI-generated outputs are interpreted on the basis of anthropocentric ideals of originality and creativity. Then, the question is not only whether certain uses of AI may infringe the copyrights of human authors, but also whether IP paradigms could technically apply to AI systems themselves, so that these might have to be recognized as authors/artists, or will, at least, challenge the integrity of prevailing perspectives on the central role and status of the human author/artist. The functionality and outputs of GANs are particularly interesting in this context, since they tend to invoke "AI creativity" very compellingly even though underlying generative processes, as I will argue, expose such systems as new kinds of highly sophisticated copy machines.

While IP law is becoming an increasingly important tool for negotiating the role of AI in the evolving socio-economic landscape, it is also becoming clear that AI can serve as a tool to elude the limits IP law has traditionally sought to impose on creative practices which involve copying activities. In this sense, AI art is in a good position to extend and expand the trajectory of appropriation art and other artistic approaches that stand opposed to the property-oriented logic of authorship, and which have long engaged critically with the reproducibility of information and aesthetic artefacts. If human artists' practices of imitation, copying, or reproduction are thought of as likely breaches of IP restrictions, then there can be no doubt that generative AI technologies are increasing the critical stakes of such practices. As I will discuss in the chapters to follow, this is already triggering interesting controversies surrounding AI-generated artworks that challenge ideas of the traditional (human) artist figure and their exclusive rights, of the nature of the work of art, and of the art market as such. AI, in other words, has the potential to substantially disturb IP policy and political economies that have formed around the romantic ideal of the author as owner.

There is now a considerable body of research that links IP theory and AI discourse, yet there is no consensus, among legal scholars and cultural theorists of AI and IP, about whether artificially intelligent systems are capable of autonomously producing the kinds of creative expression to which IP law could conventionally be applied. Widely available mainstream AI tools used for generating novel digital imagery—for example AI apps capable of style transfer (see Yuan 2018) or GAN-style image generation tools (see ArtBreeder n.d.)—seem to indicate that AI is limited, at best, to the emulation of creativity in the anthropocentric senses of the term. When Nigel Shaboldt, the co-founder of the Open Data Institute, was asked if he believed that computational systems can be creative, he is said to have deflected the question by responding, "machines will become adept at persuading us that there is indeed something behind the façade" (Miller 2019). Matteo Pasquinelli (2019), a key cultural theorist of AI, is similarly skeptical when he argues that state-of-the-art AI technologies have little to do with creativity as such, and are better understood as highly sophisticated tools for statistical analysis.

Such criticism notwithstanding, there are also those who herald the coming of truly "creative" AI. In one of several recent monographs focusing directly on this subject, the mathematician and popular science writer Marcus du Sautoy frames creativity as a kind of "human code" (2019) which, in the author's opinion, can be computed algorithmically with such efficiency that machine creativity must eclipse human creativity sooner or later. This perspective aligns problematically with what James Bridle (2018), echoing Bernard Stiegler and others, has criticized as a pervasive form of "computational thinking," i.e., the application of computational logic to efforts of solving hard problems such as developing artificial intelligence and computer-based creativity. Indeed, computational thinking goes far beyond a basic understanding of algorithmic processes as "methods for solving problems that are suited for computer implementation" (Sedgewick and Wayne 2011, 3); sometimes criticized as "computationalist," it can pander to generalizing assumptions concerning the abstractability and programmability of human behavior, in ways that ignore or overlook crucial political issues (for influential contributions to such critiques see, for example, Dougherty 2001; Hayles 2005). AI systems certainly already are what Ed Finn has called "culture machines" (2017), at least in the sense that they contribute importantly to the socio-cultural fabric in which they are embedded. But this acknowledgement says little about whether creativity should indeed be considered as "effectively computable" (cf. Copeland 2020), i.e., whether AI systems could, at least theoretically, match the creative capabilities of the current top-of-the-line culture machine, the human agent itself.

Inevitably, serious consideration of issues related to creative AI, and to computational creativity more generally, requires that some fundamental questions regarding the nature of intelligence must also be revisited. In cultural contexts, this is of course precisely what makes the concept of AI so compelling. Thus: what is meant by creativity in relation to AI, and what metaphysical, ontological, and hermeneutical frameworks are invoked to address the concept in such contexts? How do new perspectives on AI-inflected creativity function in conjunction with the prevailing mix of aesthetic theories, socio-cultural norms, economic policy, and legal regulation concerning creative expression? Zylinska suggests that in much current AI research, the underlying concept of intelligence is somewhat of a blind spot, "either taken for granted without too much interrogation or molded at will and then readjusted depending on the direction the research has taken" (2020, 19). A similar observation applies to the ways in which the concept of creativity is invoked in AI contexts, where it is defined and used across human-exclusive and AI-specific contexts. For example, two prominent researchers of creativity, the psychology and human development researcher Robert J. Sternberg and the cognitive science scholar Margaret A. Boden, rely on similar sets of criteria in their definitions of creativity (these revolve, in a nutshell, around novelty, originality, unexpectedness, and usefulness), even though Sternberg's work (2011) focuses on topics such as imagination, wisdom, and love, while Boden (1990) is a key reference for computer scientists' efforts to program creativity in computational systems. My own approach to this issue will be to adopt a mix of prevalent definitions, and accept as creative those behaviors, phenomena, activities, and artefacts that can be meaningfully interpreted as such in the aesthetic, cultural, socio-economic, and legal milieus which creativity and art are understood to inhabit (more on this in the following chapter). This, I hope, is helpful for developing a perspective that does not discriminate by default between human and nonhuman actants when navigating the diverse meanings and critical valences of creative expression in relation to digital art and AI, or, likewise, in relation to the philosophical and legal perspectives that frame them.

As I have already suggested, any claim that a given artwork was created not by a human artist but instead by an AI system must contend, at least speculatively, with the existence of an AI author/artist. If taken seriously, the notion of creative AI must then be seen to potentially undermine humanist ideals and romantic fictions of the genius artist (human, of course) and their (historically: his) unique ability to create original, inspired artworks. Given the larger context of my discussion, this is important because of how these same ideals have long served to justify and perpetuate IP models. In brief, the law tends to link intellectual ownership claims in an aesthetic artefact to the (human) individual from whom it is found to have originated. The intellectual or creative labor exerted in the production of such an artefact generally entitles its author to a range of exclusive rights. Critical uses of AI in artistic contexts can disturb the integrity of all these assumptions significantly. In other words: when an AI system isn't just understood as a tool used by human artists, but as an agential entity (or an assemblage of such entities) capable of "creative" expression, this then problematizes not only aesthetic assumptions regarding the nature of creativity and authorship, but by extension also socio-economic and legal assumptions regarding the ownership or, indeed, the very "ownability" of such expressions.

Overview

Throughout this book, the discussion of how artists working with AI link questions of creativity and agency to issues of cultural ownership forms a key part of my effort to sketch out a critical theory of AI art. As noted, my focus in this is on AI art's potential for disturbing property-oriented frameworks that emerge out of humanist perspectives. Central to this project is the observation that key underlying concepts—AI, agency, creativity, ownership—are themselves far from stable. AI art, I argue, can seize on this instability, for example in critiques of dataset bias, of AI's impact on privacy, or of algorithmic governmentality. The targets of such critiques themselves may be obscured by extreme algorithmic complexity, blackboxed in proprietary technologies, or packaged in code and algorithms that operate at a scale that is inaccessible to human cognition, or which are simply not human-readable. Digital art can cross these thresholds and give more accessible shape to these issues and the underlying technologies. As I will argue, it can do so by approaching AI tactically, by appropriating it, and by redeploying it to different, critical ends. Throughout the following chapters, I will thus discuss the becoming-tactical of AI in critical artistic practice as a development that mobilizes AI's emergent capabilities for interrogating, exposing, problematizing, and challenging the aesthetic, ideological, or technological frameworks driving the commodification and propertization of creative expression.

While this book is a fundamentally interdisciplinary endeavor, different chapters will focus on different elements of the broader discussion. This means that while the chapters add up (I hope) to a multifaceted whole that integrates arguments, problems, and perspectives from very different areas of theoretical inquiry and artistic practice, they can also be read individually. As such, chapter 2 and chapter 3 primarily (but not exclusively) deal in theory, and address ontological and definitional problems of agency, creativity, and ownership across the realms of philosophy, legal theory, and posthumanist thought. Chapter 4, chapter 5, and chapter 7 comprise in-depth analyses of separate AI art projects, to explore how these projects engage critically with the issues raised in the preceding chapters. Chapter 6 offers a counterpoint to this discussion, and considers how tactical aspects of critical AI practices can also manifest in strategic inversions, specifically in corporate AI applications in the digital culture mainstream. Chapter 8, finally, brings my discussion to a conclusion in sketching out a speculative framework for a posthumanist cultural commons that could accommodate the critical approaches to AI outlined throughout.

To offer a slightly more detailed summary: Chapter 2 begins to unpack what a critical art of AI could be. This includes theoretical elaboration on some key concepts that play into my overall project, including those of agency and creativity, as well as my attempt to define AI in the specific cultural context of contemporary digital art-making. This is framed with reference to relevant aspects of posthumanist theory, and with a more detailed introduction of my concept of the posthumanist agential assemblage, which, in the broader context of my discussion, is meant to offer a way to push AI art beyond the humanist subject of the singular, unified artist, their individualized voice, and their original and uniquely spirited creative expression. The chapter concludes with an initial discussion of tactical approaches to working with AI. This includes a brief analysis of Kate Crawford and Trevor Paglen's collaborative project *ImageNet Roulette* (2019) and its highly effective critique of dataset bias, which offers a good segue to beginning a broader critical discussion of how agency is construed in and through AI.

Chapter 3 begins with a brief discussion of Michael A. Noll's *Gaussian Quadratic* (1963), a generative work that here serves as an early example of the fraught interfacing between computer art and copyright law. This sets the stage for unpacking the interrelated foundations of agency, personhood, and ownership in legal philosophy, with a focus on theories of IP in general. Also included is a consideration of how property itself is conceived philosophically, as well as some explanatory commentary on main histories of copyright. The chapter then surveys key issues of authorship in legal research on presumptively "creative" AI, highlighting in particular the anthropocentric biases that frequently characterize such work.

Chapter 4 extends these specific concerns to an in-depth discussion of the controversy surrounding *Portrait of Edmond Belamy*

(2018), an AI-generated artwork that was auctioned off, for the record sum of US$432,500, on behalf of a French group named Obvious Collective, amidst allegations that the work's code base had actually been taken, without due credit, from the young AI artist Robbie Barrat. My focus here will be on spectacularizing claims that the work was "not the product of a human mind" but "a work of art created by an algorithm" (Christie's 2018). Several aspects of the work itself contradict this claim, which is, in fact, conceptualized and produced in problematic alignment with humanist notions of authorship and cultural ownership. In light of the informal copyright and ownership debate that the controversy provoked, I conclude this chapter by considering whether a tactical use of generative AI could render an artwork "unownable" when the use of the technology makes it difficult to recognize a conventional author figure.

In chapter 5, I explore possible answers to this question by analyzing one of the first formal copyright infringement complaints involving a work of AI art. The work in question, the Canadian artist Adam Basanta's AI-driven "art factory" *All We'd Ever Need Is One Another* (2018), serves as an excellent example of a tactical approach to working with AI. Manifesting as what I call a posthumanist agential assemblage, it affords the human artist who designed it a certain level of "deniability" of expressive agency. In other words, the use of AI here destabilizes the anthropocentric concept of authorship to such a degree that the allegations of copyright violation leveraged against Basanta by another artist may become difficult to uphold.

Chapter 6 considers the conjunction of creative expression, AI, and the destabilization of authorship in a broader context. Temporarily stepping away from discussion of AI-driven digital art, in this chapter I analyze Content ID, the AI-based digital rights management system used by YouTube to enforce its copyright policy. In this context, the potential deniability of creative agency emerges not as an artistic choice (as in the previous chapter), but instead as a highly problematic curtailment. As I argue, Content

ID shifts away from an enactment of emerging non-human agency in AI, and instead reorients itself toward the enforcing of human non-agency through AI. Again, this has far-reaching implications for how notions of authorship, ownership, and agency play out at the intersection of humans and AI.

Integrating insights and arguments from the preceding chapter, chapter 7 speculates on a broader-scale becoming-tactical of AI art, and considers in more depth some critical implications of the destabilization of humanist ideals in and through posthumanist agential assemblages. This discussion begins with an analysis of two projects by the British AI artist Jake Elwes, *Machine Learning Porn* (2016) and *Zizi* (2019), both of which enact a deliberate "queering" of AI and dataset politics. Foregrounding the dynamism of sexual identity and invoking issues of cultural ownership, these works draw on AI to problematize normative, anthropocentric discourse on established subject positions. My final example, *!brute_force*, is an ongoing project by the Slovenian artist Maja Smrekar, which introduces canine intelligence into an experimental AI training regimen in order to explore co-constitutive qualities of human and non-human ontologies of agency and knowledge production. A powerful example of a posthumanist agential assemblage, *!brute_force* goes to considerable lengths to create speculative systems of decentered, relational, and contingent subject positions, with the effect that questions of agency and cultural ownership are reconfigured beyond anthropocentric horizons.

From the co-constitutive human-AI-canine knowledge ontologies envisioned in *!brute_force* to the defamiliarizing appropriation of AI functionality in *Zizi*, from the legal provocations of *All We'd Ever Need Is One Another* to the clumsy declamations of non-human creative agency in *Portrait of Edmond Belamy*, and from the uncloaking of AI bias in *ImageNet Roulette* to the problematic enactment of human non-agency in the Content ID system—what commonalities, productive contradictions, and critical potentialities reverberate across the examples discussed throughout this book? The final chapter considers the new conceptual space that is constituted by the becoming-tactical of AI in posthumanist agential assemblages. In revisiting my earlier suggestions that certain uses and outputs of presumptively agential AI can be fundamentally incompatible with anthropocentric perspectives on creativity, originality, and authorship, I conclude by sketching out the concept of a posthumanist cultural commons, and by considering how—and to what critical ends—such a commons could contain the works and workings of the posthumanist agential assemblage.

[2]

What Does AI Hack? Scaffolding for a Critical Art of AI

My aim in this chapter is to consider in more detail what a critical art of AI could be. This entails some additional unpacking of key concepts that play into my project, including those of agency, creativity, and the notion of AI itself. Framing this discussion with reference to contemporary perspectives on agency as fundamentally relational and distributed then leads me to introduce the concept of the posthumanist agential assemblage. Throughout this book, this concept will offer a way of exploring AI art and its critical implications beyond the humanist subject, and without having to rely on the restrictive conceptual framing of the traditionally singular, unified artist figure, their individualized voice, or the original and uniquely spirited creative expression. To locate AI art in the works and workings of the posthumanist agential assemblage also makes it easier to specify how a critical art of AI may disturb property-oriented frameworks derived from humanist perspectives. This initial discussion of the posthumanist agential assemblage sets the stage for exploring, in the next chapter, how questions of AI agency play out in legal theory, where they connect much more directly to issues of authorship, personhood, and ownership. Following a brief discussion of Kate Crawford and Trevor Paglen's critical AI art project *ImageNet Roulette* (2019), I conclude this chapter by defining what I will call "tactical" approaches to utilizing AI in artistic practice. Not all of the AI art projects discussed later on constitute posthumanist agential assemblages, nor do all of them operate in a tactical mode; all of them, however, will be considered in relation to these concepts, and the speculative horizon of a critical art of AI as it is laid out here.

To begin, I want to argue that to engage critically with AI, whether in digital art or in a theoretical capacity, is likely going to involve a conceptual and/or practical "hacking" of AI. For example, in a call for proposals for a workshop held at the 2020 Transmediale Festival, contributors were invited to adopt an "adversarial" approach, and "break into the technological abstractions of AI" (Transmediale n.d.) in order to consider what it might mean to produce new knowledge and critical literacies about artificial intelligence. Similarly, *Ways of Machine Seeing* and *Machine Feeling*, two event series organized at Cambridge University's Centre for Research in the Arts, Social Sciences, and Humanities (CRASSH) between 2017 and 2019, sought to integrate practical and critical approaches co-developed by computer scientists, researchers, and artists, and encouraged critiques of AI that may also directly utilize the technology (see Impett 2017; Andersen and Cox 2019). I fully agree that AI, like all emerging technologies, should be subject to every manner of hacking efforts by activists, artists, researchers, engineers, and so on. It should be subjected, in other words, to theory- and practice-based structural analysis and ideological critiques that may materialize in speculative alternatives to existing AI implementation and development approaches. It strikes me that a good point of departure for doing this is to approach the issue from an inverse angle—by asking what is already being hacked in conventional uses of AI, or, to put it differently, what AI as such is capable of hacking. Among the art projects discussed in the following chapters, several approach AI from precisely this kind of angle, and go on to explore what hacks are in turn made possible by divergent uses of AI.

To elaborate some observations and arguments already introduced in the previous chapter, I begin my discussion of critical AI art by offering two speculative claims concerning artificial intelligence, which converge in a third: AI hacks agency, AI hacks creativity, and AI hacks ownership. (All three require a fairly self-evident disclaimer, namely that these hacks are not achieved, of course, by AI "itself," but rather through practices that AI technologies facilitate.) In the most straightforward sense, the first claim, that AI hacks agency, can mean that AI is becoming a standard element of algorithmic control regimes. The validity of this claim is easy to test in various contexts, including the AI-driven manipulation of consumer behavior (e.g., recommendation algorithms), the state-level use of facial recognition technologies, or the use of AI-based predictive technologies in the financial and insurance sector. In all of these areas, human agents' ability of self-determination and politically informed expression—what Bernard Stiegler, in his last book, called "dreaming" (Stiegler 2019)—are impacted and, to varying degrees, curtailed. This links to the second claim, namely that AI hacks creativity. By this I mean that emerging AI technologies impact how creativity is defined in a general sense, how specific creative practices are reconfigured as a result, and how shifts in the production and circulation of creative expression are consequently negotiated and regulated. All of this manifests, for example, in debates around whether AI and its outputs could be claimed to be creative (or to be capable of becoming creative).

Where these two claims regarding the hacking capabilities of AI converge, a third can be formulated, namely that AI hacks ownership. In other words, a potential becoming-agential and becoming-creative of AI challenges key assumptions regarding humanist foundations of the concept of authorship and the nature of the work of art, and by extension also assumptions concerning how these foundations underpin current IP regimes.

For one thing, speculation on the emergence of artistic AI systems that could soon compete with human artists suggests that it may become more challenging to assign authorship (and enforce ownership rights), and therefore also to maintain the integrity of these concepts. For another, ongoing efforts to make creativity machine-readable can enable AI systems to interpret, validate, and consequently control how creative expression circulates digitally. This can already be observed in examples such as the use of AI-based digital rights management (DRM) tools for enforcing corporate copyright policy (the main topic of chapter 6). As a consequence, the ability of a given agent (whether human or non-human) to express themselves creatively and critically, to access knowledge and information as part of expressive activities, and to participate freely in the production and circulation of art and culture, could be severely impinged. It is here that AI's impact on the question of agency and of creativity links most directly to current IP models. As I will argue, the various hacking capabilities of AI can be utilized strategically, i.e., in alignment with such models, but also in opposition to them. I describe the latter as tactical uses of AI, and will conclude the chapter by elaborating this notion, both as an extension of existing discourse on tactical media, and in the context of the kinds of critical AI art projects discussed throughout the book.

Redefining AI in and through Artistic Practice

AI is a strange, chimera-like beast. Arguably, it is as much a science as it is a technology, as much a cultural phenomenon as it is a philosophical construct. And while AI can be said, quite plausibly, to be all of those things, it may also be argued that it is really just mythical fabulation, that it does not exist at all. While some argue that what is now called AI will continue to inch closer to a full exteriorization of "general intelligence," and then on toward a "singularity" event (Kurzweil 2005), others insist that AI will remain a computational augmentation of human intelligence (as discussed in Markoff 2015). The difficulty of definitively describing artificial intelligence is also complicated by the so-called "AI effect." This occurs when technological advances lead to newly emerging behaviors of AI systems that would once have been thought of as proof of intelligence, but which are no longer accepted as such because the underlying computational processes are understood better (cf. McCorduck 2004). In other words, as the capabilities of specific AI applications are moving into the mainstream or are superseded by new developments, they are no longer seen as satisfying existing definitions of intelligent behavior, so that AI always remains an elusive "n+1". At the 2019 Ars Electronica festival, the media art historian Andreas Broeckmann suggested that it might indeed be best to use scare quotes whenever "artificial intelligence" is invoked, while the media theorist Joanna Zylinska describes much of AI as "a so-called intelligence" (2020).

But regardless of how broadly or narrowly AI is conceived, and regardless of whether "Artificial General Intelligence" (AGI) is framed anthropocentrically in terms of "true," "strong," or "weak," or rather as something that human intelligence cannot even begin to fathom, there are some general characteristics that find broader, interdisciplinary agreement. For example, a general definition of AI that integrates widely held perspectives from the technical and social sciences as well as the humanities is likely to focus on the description of algorithmic tools that are capable of generating knowledge of some kind, often on the basis of iterative and generative processes that involve large-scale analysis of datasets on which AI systems are trained. It is also generally accepted that machine learning technologies are increasingly responsible for how humans perceive the world, how they interact with it, and, consequently, who (and how) human agents can be in a world with AI. Definitions nevertheless diverge widely across different research domains. An influential definition by Russell and Norvig (2009) hints at this divergence nicely: their definition situates AI in a four-dimensional spectrum to consider whether any given "intelligent agent" is designed to think (or act) like humans, or, rather, to think (or act) rationally. While the work of Russell and Norvig has tended to focus on rational (non-human-based) action (as opposed to thinking), the authors acknowledge that more informally, the term AI is often used to describe systems that cross over between these definitional boundaries in direct imitation of functions associated with human cognition. Notably, all of this leaves considerable room for very different kinds of philosophical, technical, and ideological viewpoints.

To extend these broad characterizations into the cultural sphere and connect them to my discussion of critical artistic practice, I venture the following definition of AI: I will describe as artificially intelligent any assemblage of technologies, operations, functions, and effects that can be meaningfully perceived as resulting from intelligent (including creative) behavior, or which can be identified in outputs that are the results of such behavior. This formulation is deliberately inclusive, open-ended, and focused on perception. While it allows for the designation "AI"—with or without scare quotes—to be applied to technological systems such as advanced computational neural networks that approximate functions of the human brain, it can also describe the effects created when the behaviors of an otherwise dull machinic system are perceived as intelligent, or when its outputs are interpreted as creative. My definition therefore acknowledges that while inevitably there must be a non-human dimension to artificial intelligence, AI is nevertheless contingent upon human perception and interpretation. Much like the co-originary nature of the human and the technical (cf. Stiegler 1998), AI is, in other words, co-constitutive with human intelligence. Further, because my discussion is framed by an interest in how AI interfaces with realms of art, culture, and politics, my perspective disregards the notion of AI as unfathomable for human cognition, and I emphasize, instead, that AI is in the eye of the beholder. Even so, my definition is positioned both against the anthropomorphizing of AI as human-like, and against anthropocentrically biased definitions that perceive AI as existing in a position of subservience to human users. Importantly, I also want to avoid thinking of AI as bounded in any singular entity, such as an algorithm or a computer. This helps to accommodate the many ways in which AI is continually rethought, redefined, and newly instantiated in and across emerging technologies, new tools, as well as new ways of using and critiquing these. Most importantly, this leaves room for a final core element of my thinking on AI, namely that it can be understood to manifest in posthumanist agential assemblages that cut across human/non-human divides, and which may incorporate human (and other living) entities alongside computational or machinic ones.

A broad definition such as the one just offered isn't likely to satisfy everyone. Much more precise definitions can be found in virtually every field of research on which my own discussion draws, from philosophy to computational creativity, from aesthetic theory to legal philosophy. My definition has the advantage, however, that it can accommodate the broader interdisciplinary focus through which I link agency and ownership issues to AI. Where necessary and useful, my broad conception of AI will, in any case, solidify into much more specific definitions, for example when discussing how artists use machine learning technologies such as Generative Adversarial Networks (GANs), or when considering the blackboxing of proprietary algorithms used for digital rights management (DRM) purposes. Ultimately, dipping in and out of the wide range of available technical definitions of AI makes it easier to connect them to the philosophical, aesthetic, legal, and political strands of my discussion, and to show how this can be incorporated into the self-reflexive and meta-discursive critiques that critical AI art leverages.

In discussions of AI, it is sometimes far from clear what exactly "intelligence" itself signifies. It might be objected, for example, that my own definition of AI can accommodate not only "true" intelligence (however that might be construed), but that it could also apply to the mere imitation or simulation of intelligent behaviors or effects. Such a concern was well articulated in the philosopher John Searle's famous "Chinese Room" argument (cf. Searle 1980 and Cole 2020), which concerned the difficulty of differentiating between the correct-but-meaningless manipulation of linguistic symbols and an actual understanding of these symbols. The thought experiment describes how an entity, concealed in a room, might convince an observer on the outside that it knows the Chinese language, even though it remains impossible for the observer to determine whether this knowledge expresses intelligence or merely a mute ability to convincingly simulate intelligence.

Importantly, this distinction loses much of its relevance when the focus is placed simply on whether the entity concealed in the room can be perceived, for all intents and purposes, as displaying intelligent behavior. Even if true non-human intelligence were understood as being so profoundly different from our own that it could become unknowable for humans (as discussed in Bown 2015 and Bridle 2018, among others), what Searle's example suggests is that I can only ever relate to AI through an inflection of my own, inevitably human-centric, understanding of what determines intelligence. In the baseline definition of AI that I have proposed above, it is for this reason that to identify AI means to interpret perceivable functions, effects, or behaviors as intelligent. This acknowledges that the theoretical frameworks I invoke are themselves interpretive paradigms, and it highlights that I am, of course, speaking from the perspective of human agency. To acknowledge this is also to open up AI toward the integration of posthumanist thought, where, as I discuss below, the agencies in which "intelligence" is grounded are understood as relational, dynamic, and multi-dimensional.

I have noted earlier that anthropocentric configurations of AI may manifest in surveillance technology, in financial applications, and in new algorithmic legal tools, where they build on and, indeed, amplify ideological frameworks that privilege (and also exploit) the human agent and the presumptively singular subject position it is often understood to inhabit. Key to my overall discussion is the observation that something similar applies when presumptively "creative" AI is framed in anthropocentric terms that derive from longstanding notions of the singular, unified artist figure: the anthropocentric instrumentalization of AI in copyright contexts, for example, will ever only be able to enforce IP perspectives in which the human author/artist figure functions as the singular originator and proprietor of human-made creative expression. Such an instrumentalization could hardly accommodate non-human authorship of—or ownership in—creative expressions.

To elucidate this, I offer two brief examples that will undergo closer analysis in subsequent chapters. The first concerns the Canadian artist Adam Basanta's AI-driven installation *All We'd Ever Need Is One Another* (2018). Building on approaches familiar from appropriation art, the installation is designed to autonomously generate outputs and to circulate them as artworks if, and only if, they are determined by an AI system to closely resemble other existing artworks (see chapter 5). While this approach aligns with progressive views on creativity as multi-modal and relational, unsurprisingly it contradicts perspectives that are focused on identifying single (human) authors for unique artworks. And indeed, *All We'd Ever Need Is One Another* has provoked a legal complaint alleging that the installation violates another artist's IP rights. Given the prominent role of AI in the generative process, my discussion of this case speculates that Basanta himself cannot be credibly accused of copyright infringement, and I argue that the accusation itself makes sense only as long as it hinges on an anthropocentric perspective on AI, authorship, and creativity. The second example is situated at the interstices between creative expression and commercial AI applications, and concerns YouTube's AI-driven DRM system Content ID (see chapter 6). This tool is designed to flag and remove presumptively infringing media uploads by enforcing the assumption that creative expression is incontrovertibly linked to ownership claims based on identifiable human authorship. By enacting this view algorithmically, Content ID helps to integrate uploads into the platform's for-profit, property-oriented media ecology. Additionally, it normalizes the highly problematic notion that complex legal norms concerning authorship, which are themselves intimately tied to long histories of philosophical discourse on the subject, are effectively computable. On this basis, Content ID disavows more complex configurations of creative expression and agency, which it consequently prevents from freely circulating.

The example of Content ID indicates that AI is capable of enforcing the notion of singular human agency, and in doing so of impeding divergent forms of creative expression that draw on relational, multi-modal, recombinant models. The example of *All We'd Ever Need Is One Another*, in turn, suggests that AI experiments which go beyond the anthropocentric paradigm of singular human creative agency can disturb the logic of the ownership models which systems such as Content ID are designed to safeguard. The project frames a new kind of AI-driven creative expression that no longer fits (conceptually or practically) with the familiar idea of unique expressions that are uniquely linked to artists/authors/owners, and which effectively challenges anthropocentric ownership models that tend to be amplified in current AI applications. My discussion of this kind of AI art espouses a move toward a position that does not privilege human agency above its various non-human interlocutors, and in this sense Basanta's project will serve as a good example of what I describe as a posthumanist agential assemblage.

Whence and Whither Agency?

In all of this, agency reveals itself as a rather slippery idea. There are numerous ways in which the concept has been defined across different strands of philosophy, law, psychology, and neuroscience—not to mention poststructuralism, actor-network theory, postcolonial theory, feminist theory, and queer theory, among others. Most basically, agency denotes the manifestation of a capacity to act (see, for example, Schlosser 2019, on which this brief summary in part relies, and Chopra and White 2011, who try to develop a legal theory of autonomous artificial agents). But things quickly get a lot more complicated. Contemporary philosophical perspectives on agency tend to take as a common starting point the "standard theory of action" (cf. Davidson 1980), which considers actions in terms of their intentionality. The theory assumes that an entity is capable of exercising agency if it is also capable of acting intentionally. In more detailed analyses of intentionality that also consider causation, will, or motivation, this leads onwards to theories of distinctly human agency (e.g., Frankfurt 1971; Taylor 1977). By some accounts, then, a human agent is simply a human who acts. But further obstacles appear when additional underlying questions are considered: What is an "agent," in this sense, and what defines an "action"? What level of autonomy is required to warrant the designation "agential"? Who or what can be the judge of intentionality? Once agency becomes vested in human beings, it also becomes necessary to ascribe and account for mental states, as well as to consider socio-political dimensions of autonomy, conscious deliberation, and reasoning. It is here that human agency can easily become separated hierarchically from other, non-human forms of agency, resulting in a normative formalization of anthropocentric bias. Therefore, when the agency of artificially intelligent entities is considered, the standard theory of action, with its strong focus on intentionality and, by extension, mental states, becomes somewhat of a hindrance, rather than an aid, with the consequence that advanced AI systems might inevitably be relegated to the "lower" status of mere "minimally agential" entities (e.g., Barandiaran et al. 2009).

The views on agency I have presented so far are limited in the sense that they leave little room for considering the political dimensions of agency in socio-economic contexts. Their applicability to AI systems is also limited, and they certainly cannot easily account for an understanding of AI systems as "culture machines" that reach beyond anthropocentric paradigms. In this sense, it is the idea of AI itself that casts doubt on the centrality of the human when it comes to questions of agency. This notion reverberates powerfully through post-humanist perspectives. Here, agency is no longer perceived as the exclusive domain of human subjectivity, nor even of animate bodies. Bruno Latour, for example, in formulating his actor-network theory (ANT), heralded the use of the term "actant," which he defined as "something that acts or to which activity is granted by others," and which "implies *no* special motivation of *human individual* actors, nor of humans in general" (Latour 1996, 373, emphasis in original). New materialism, to give a different example, ascribes "vitality" to inanimate matter that has the capacity, as Jane Bennett writes, "not only to impede or block the will and designs of humans, but also to act as quasi agents or forces with trajectories, propensities, or tendencies of their own" (Bennett 2009, viii). In extending these perspectives, some posthumanist strands of thought altogether veer away from the notion of a unified and singular host of agency, and instead foreground the fluidity and open-endedness of the assemblage or apparatus that comes to replace the once-singular agent. The quantum physicist and feminist theorist Karen Barad (2007) thus proposes an "agential realism" in which agency radiates not from a singular host but emerges through "intra-actional" entanglements that cut across the various materialities which form agential potentials. In much of this, boundaries between the human and non-human are entirely rejected, and unsurprisingly, this also broadly rejects humanist attitudes inscribed in familiar anthropocentric figurations of agency (cf. Braidotti 2013).

Taken together, these perspectives contest the notion of agency as clearly delineated, stable, and singularly grounded in the human subject. Agency here becomes relational, porous, fluid, and distributed. Where humanist and anthropocentric perspectives persist, they take form, for example, in the legal status of personhood. As a specific instantiation of (mostly) human agency, this anchors many of the rights and responsibilities of contemporary agential subjects, from the right to free expression to the ability to own property. But here, the dynamism and inclusivity of posthumanist perspectives is nowhere yet to be found (unless one were inclined to accept the concept of corporate personhood as a radical decentering of human subjectivity). What is noticeable, however, is that anthropocentrically conceived norms and limits of agency are today increasingly upheld through AI technologies that are also potentially capable, as I argue, to disturb these same norms and limits. I have already mentioned examples of how non-human, computational entities can be instrumentalized to perpetuate narrow conceptions of agency in surveillance, governance, and IP contexts. It is precisely against this backdrop that AI must be engaged critically, to rethink what is meant by agency as such, and to explore radical implications of non-human expressive agency enacted through AI. The speculative scattering of agency across human-machinic-algorithmic assemblages instantiated in critical artistic experiments with AI are an ideal vehicle for just this kind of rethinking.

It is here that the critical potential of the posthumanist agential assemblage becomes more apparent. The concept offers a way to push AI—and AI art—beyond the humanist subject of the singular, unified artist, their individualized voice, and their original and uniquely spirited creative expression. In the works created by and with such assemblages, the artwork loses its humanist contours, while the dynamism and relationality of creative expression become manifest. And in their workings—in the operational logic, functionality, routines, protocols, and processes that characterize AI—the productive entanglements between different human and non-human elements find expression in manifold redistributions of agency across all participating elements. The works and workings of the posthumanist agential assemblage will continue to take shape throughout the following chapters. What all of the examples will be found to share is that they engage critically with the humanist horizons of a singular, unified agency and the various frameworks of cultural ownership and intellectual property that rely on these.

In making the leap from intelligence to creativity, it is worth looking a bit more closely at the entanglements of AI and agency in the Turing test, as well as a few of its successors-in-spirit. Alan Turing (1950) proposed his original test as a hypothesis concerning how human observers might identify a computer system as intelligent. Right away, the test's most notable characteristic should be emphasized here, namely that to identify a computer system as intelligent means to mistake it for another human agent. While Turing's setup is ingeniously simple, it also hinges centrally on a fairly obvious expression of anthropocentric bias. In response to this, as well as to eliminate how the Turing test potentially endorses the mere simulation of intelligence, Selmer Bringsjord et al. (2001) designed the hypothetical Lovelace test, which proposes that a computational system can be accepted as intelligent when it is capable of producing outputs that human observers will interpret as creative expressions. Bringsjord et al.'s test builds on Ada Lovelace's oft-cited suggestion that computers cannot be said to possess intelligence because they "have no pretensions whatever to originate anything" (Lovelace, quoted in Baum 1986). It tests, in other words, for qualities which computers, according to Ada Lovelace, cannot possess. In this setup, a human observer is tasked with judging whether the presumptively artistic output of a computer is, indeed, creative. This is found to be the case if the human observer cannot explain how an output was generated, even when it is verifiably not based on a mere hardware error (Bringsjord et al. 2001, 9). Like Lovelace herself, Bringsjord and his co-authors assume that this is effectively impossible, and conclude that (at the time of their writing) the hypothetical test was not likely to be beaten by any computer, in part because the machine would need to possess a "rather radical kind of autonomy" that they find difficult to imagine, let alone to design (ibid. 25).

The ambition of the Lovelace test is to improve upon some of the Turing test's perceived flaws, in part by replacing a judge's subjectivity with a query regarding the algorithmic foundations underlying presumptively creative AI outputs. But it can be argued that the test merely replaces one subjective notion (an anthropocentric understanding of intelligence) with another (an anthropocentric understanding of creativity). This criticism can also be applied to more recent iterations of the Lovelace test. For example, based on the assumption that human creativity is fundamentally rule-driven and algorithmic, Marcus du Sautoy (2019) proposes his own Lovelace test, which is virtually identical to the version of Bringsjord et al. except for the slight twist that it should also be repeatable, i.e., not random. Lev Manovich's Turing AI Arts test, to give a different example, shares the goal of the Lovelace test(s) before it, but is modeled more directly on Turing's test design. Problematically, Manovich adds an elitist dimension to the anthropocentric bias of the original: in this version, the artistic nature of AI outputs is asserted only when "professional members of the art world recognize [them] as belonging to 'contemporary art'" (2019, 1). What these proposed tests share is that their determinations of non-human creativity and intelligence are made on the assumption that all creativity and/or intelligence will resemble that of human agents. They all propose that if the test is passed, the non-human entities that are being evaluated are elevated to a realm of agency that renders them, oddly, more human-like. Again, I would argue that such a perspective can hardly accommodate dynamic and relational manifestations of agency in a posthumanist sense, nor new forms of perceived intelligence or creativity that these could frame.

In this context, "pretensions" and "originate" jump out from the Lovelace statement quoted above. The terms imply that if an AI system were capable of passing the test, it would exhibit the intention of creating outputs *ex nihilo*. This not only invokes the interrelated humanist notions of creativity, originality, and authorship, but also links to the ways in which IP theory has conventionally defined the terms, for example for the purpose of determining the copyrightability of an expression. The privileging of a will to effect originality as a core prerequisite for creative agency is also implied by Bringsjord et al.'s formulation that AI creativity must satisfy the criterion of "unexplainability." In current AI discourse, the concept of unexplainability invokes the idea that the nature of non-human intelligence (as well as the internal processes that lead to AI-generated outputs) may be unknowable from a human perspective. But when it is linked back to debates about AI creativity, the concept of unexplainability also invokes humanist ideals of authorial agency.

An important development in the trajectory from Turing test to Lovelace test is that more recent perspectives no longer seem to focus merely on identifying intelligence as such, but also on the idea that creative expression may be understood as an embodied and authentic manifestation of agency. The idea that creativity is an important marker of intelligence certainly seems valid; what is problematic is that the various tests introduced above appear to suggest either that creativity is effectively computable, or that it must be framed anthropocentrically. In any case, it would appear that, following this trajectory, it can be assumed that if AI is found to be creative, it must also be found to have agency. If it is further assumed that creative agency will be exteriorized in a form that can be grasped and evaluated by human observers (namely in presumptively creative AI-generated expressions), then inevitably there also arise difficult questions concerning the moral, legal, and economic statuses which AI-as-artist (as opposed to the human artist working with AI) and the AI-generated artwork might have to be granted.

The question of whether AI can be creative interests me only insofar as it represents an opportunity to rethink what is actually meant by creativity, and how such a rethinking can impact the technological, socio-economic, legal, and, ultimately, ideological entanglements of emerging forms and constellations of creative agency. Since creative agency implies authorship, any assumption that AI can be creative is a return to the third claim introduced at the beginning of this chapter, namely that AI is capable of hacking ownership, anthropocentrically conceived. It must therefore also be asked what ownership itself signifies in the context of agential AI. The conceptual underpinnings of the IP paradigms currently in place would seem to suggest that if AI can achieve human-like creativity, it should also be entitled, like a human author, to control the fruits of its labor. In mainstream debate on creative AI and AI art, the alarmist response to this suggestion tends to be that AI will disrupt the art market (see my discussion in chapter 4). I would argue that this should not be taken to mean only that AI will begin to "compete" with human authors, but also that critical AI art has a powerful opportunity to upend the value propositions of anthropocentric and humanist approaches to authorship. This can happen, for example, by emphasizing relational reconfigurations of agency and creative expression that move toward a decentering of the humanist (and human) subject that grounds anthropocentric property models.

The concept of property itself, even when it is narrowly conceived, always delineates a relational constellation (between owner and property, and between owners of property). Additionally, any notion of a property enclosure also entails, at least speculatively, the potential for a commons (I will return to this in my final chapter). As such, property rights, despite their notional exclusivity, are mostly situated in environments that delineate ownership as porous and malleable. The logic of IP, for example, situates copyright as a core mechanism through which the expressive agency of individuals solidifies into exclusive property rights. But this logic is recursive, since it is itself based on philosophical traditions (including Hegel's personality theory, discussed in the next chapter) that construe property as that which helps to solidify individuality, personhood, and thus agency. When critical uses of AI propose the emergence of posthumanist expressive agency, this effectively begins to undermine the recursive logic of IP.

Tactical AI

A critical art of artificial intelligence appropriates AI's capability of hacking agency, creativity, and ownership, and opposes it tactically. In doing so it strongly contrasts with what I would describe as strategic uses of AI. The distinction between strategic and tactical practices has been most prominently theorized in Michel de Certeau's *Practice of Everyday Life* (2011). De Certeau's discussion of tactics in cultural contexts has greatly influenced the work of new media art activists such as the Critical Art Ensemble (2001), and even though the concept of tactical media, as theorized, for example, by Rita Riley (2009), fell out of fashion relatively quickly, de Certeau's concept of tactics continues to resonate with a broader canon of media theoretical work from the left, for example Alexander Galloway's (2004) discussion of control protocols in decentralized communication technology, McKenzie Wark's influential *A Hacker Manifesto* (2004), or more recently the manifesto published by the Critical Engineering Working Group (Oliver et al. n.d.).

In de Certeau's formulation, the purpose of strategy is to serve administrative and managerial agendas by drawing on system-inherent control architectures, often with the purpose of containing critical or divergent elements within a system. Examples might include the organization of work processes on a shop floor, or the algorithmic ordering of consumer behavior. Strategy is described as goal-oriented, and focuses on instrumentalizing the structural affordances of the environmental/social/technological substrate in which it is embedded. In this sense, strategic approaches to AI (and perhaps even strategic critiques of it) are likely to align with what I have earlier discussed as computational thinking, and strategic implementations of AI might manifest, for example, in applications that reinforce or amplify anthropocentric ideological frameworks in surveillance, finance, or IP contexts. In artistic contexts, strategic utilization of AI may employ the technology to reinscribe anthropocentric configurations of the humanist artist figure and artwork. As examples, I would count AI works such as *Contrapposto*, discussed in the introductory chapter, as well as *Portrait of Edmond Belamy*, which is the subject of my analysis in chapter 4.

Tactics, by contrast, are described by de Certeau as the recalcitrant and oppositional response to strategic operations. In de Certeau's thinking, to proceed tactically is to practice the "art of making-do," i.e., to operate from a position that is responsive, fluid, and embedded in the system or technology that is being challenged. In comparison to strategy, tactics is less goal-oriented. It operates along open-ended vectors of resistance, rather than pursuing the ossification of a situation in strategically advantageous positions of dominance. As such, tactical approaches are associated with oppositional viewpoints, cunning, and shrewdness (see Scott 1998, discussed in Zeilinger 2017). In AI contexts, this can translate into approaches that "hack" AI in precisely the ways introduced earlier in this chapter. Tactical AI, in this sense, is likely to resist strategic approaches that blackbox knowledge, restrict access, or reinforce narrow conceptualizations of agency. In the given context of my general project, this also means that tactical approaches to working with AI align themselves with characteristics of the posthumanist agential assemblage, specifically its challenges to humanist frameworks of singular, unified agency and anthropocentric perspectives on cultural ownership.

Kate Crawford and Trevor Paglen's *ImageNet Roulette* (2019) is a good example of a critical work of AI art that proceeds tactically. Utilizing mainstream image recognition technology, the project was designed to expose bias inherent in the data used for machine learning purposes, and consequently also in the algorithmic procedures derived from them. As such, the project articulates a powerful critique of how agency and cultural ownership are construed in and through such systems (Crawford and Paglen 2019b). *ImageNet Roulette* (which, for reasons explained below, is no longer available for online viewing or use) took the form of a web interface that invited users to upload a self-portrait, which would then be evaluated and interpreted by a purpose-built image recognition system. This system had been trained on the ImageNet dataset, a compilation of over 14 million labelled images that includes everyday objects as well as portraits of individuals, and which is widely used for the development of machine vision applications by researchers, government agencies, and in corporate contexts (ImageNet 2016). Importantly, the initial labelling of the dataset contents had been carried out by clickworkers, (individuals who typically receive extremely low per-task remuneration for repetitive data-entry activities carried out remotely). The experience of interacting with *ImageNet Roulette* somewhat resembled the popular personality quiz apps that circulate on social media; in return for private user information, such apps customarily offer free and exhilarating feedback, such as pseudo-psychological profiles or astrological advice. Often, such offerings disguise app developers' ulterior motives of data-extraction for commercial or political purposes. In the case of *ImageNet Roulette*, a user's reward for uploading an image of themselves was to have the system analyze and evaluate the uploaded image, to potentially shocking effect.

The intention behind *ImageNet Roulette* was that as part of this evaluation process, it would become clear to the user that beyond the artifice of presumptively objective computational processes, artificially intelligent systems are in fact deeply saturated with human bias. The subjectivity and extreme bias ingrained in the ImageNet dataset meant that a "photograph of a woman smiling in a bikini" might be classified as a "slattern, slut, slovenly woman, trollop" (Crawford and Paglen, 2019b). To give another example, in a review of the project for *The Guardian*, a journalist of Asian descent found herself identified as "gook, slant-eye" (Wong 2019). By subjecting users to this kind of system-inherent offensive feedback, *ImageNet Roulette* very successfully managed to challenge popular assumptions regarding the presumptive objectivity and interpretive validity of computational processes;

to expose such processes, which are commonly blackboxed or otherwise not human-readable; to raise awareness of the exploitative labor practices behind biased labelling practices; to highlight data mining practices that link machine learning and private user information; and, by implication, to raise ownership issues related to dataset compilation practices and "big data" more generally.

Exposure to the hard-coded bias of the ImageNet dataset confronted users of *ImageNet Roulette* with the realization that outputs generated by non-human computational systems still express the all-too human prejudices injected into such systems, and that these systems are themselves part and parcel of the ideological frameworks that produce them and within which they circulate. In the context of discussing tactical approaches to AI, the achievement of Crawford and Paglen's project is to radically disturb the public image of machine learning technologies by appropriating and repurposing the data that forms the subject of the critique. As such, the project made it easy for non-specialist users to grasp that while the non-human, algorithmic evaluation of image characteristics cannot avoid human bias, such technology is certainly a good way of obfuscating and disguising this bias.

ImageNet Roulette thus forced an awareness that presumptively agential algorithmic systems can powerfully deny human users their own agency; in the case of this project, the evaluations received in response to uploading an image were likely to violate a user's sense of ownership with regard to their self-image, identity, and the interpretation thereof. Like the AI-based evaluative tools mimicked by *ImageNet Roulette*, the project itself flaunted a seemingly objective capability to produce new and valid knowledge about human users. But because *ImageNet Roulette* simultaneously worked to undermine this appearance, it also activated users' resistance to the workings and outputs of ImageNet.

In publications and promotional material framing the project, Crawford and Paglen raised awareness concerning the potential misappropriation of image content circulating online, specifically with regard to the web-scraping of dataset contents, a practice that frequently exploits legal loopholes in existing IP frameworks. Again, *ImageNet Roulette* approached this subject tactically, by emulating the functionality of popular online tools offering free services in return for permission to use private user data. While *ImageNet Roulette* itself was explicit about not retaining copies of uploaded images, the project format nevertheless drew attention to image ownership questions concerning the underlying dataset. For example, while the operators of ImageNet (the project is maintained in a collaboration between Princeton University and Stanford University) state that they do not hold copyrights in any of the images in the dataset, this does not mean that the individuals captured in the dataset images have consented to their use. Originally, online documentation for the project noted that ImageNet recognizes copyrights held in "the images in their original resolutions" (ImageNet Download FAQ). But this implied that the institutions maintaining the project may well claim ownership in the collections of low-resolution thumbnails with which labels and classifiers are paired, or likewise in the compilation of URLs linking back to the original images. Additionally, the project website clarifies that copies of all images in the dataset are kept on non-public servers, where they can be made available, upon request, for certain non-commercial and/or educational uses. While this formulation suggests that ImageNet is not meant for commercial exploitation, it is very difficult to control the contexts within which tools derived from ImageNet are used.

The achievements of *ImageNet Roulette* consist in the efficiency with which the project reconfigured the existing structure and functionality of ImageNet into a powerful critique of the underlying technology, as well as in the impact that the project had on public perceptions of dataset bias. As such, the project exemplifies how tactical artistic approaches can disturb, complicate, and contest problematic ideological figurations of AI, and offers a good context for beginning to explore how agency is construed in and through AI. Within less than a year of the project's release, hundreds of thousands of images and image descriptors were being removed from the ImageNet dataset (see Yang et al. 2019; Rea 2019), at which point the project was taken offline.

Tactical uses of AI, as I have described them above, denote critical modes of practice that proceed along vectors of flexibility, deterritorialization, and resilience. In contrast to the computational thinking encoded in strategic AI (such as ImageNet itself), tactical AI ultimately emphasizes the need for broader systemic understanding in computational contexts. It exemplifies a push toward what Bridle calls a fluency "not only in the language of a system, but in its metalanguage" (2018). Arguably, *ImageNet Roulette* aimed to steer its users toward such a critical systemic literacy of AI. Ed Finn describes this as the ability to develop practices of "algorithmic reading," i.e., the ability to develop and implement a "critical frame for interpreting objects that are also interpreting you" (Finn 2017, 55). In the following chapters, I will expand my discussion of AI art to projects which, like *ImageNet Roulette*, address issues of agency and cultural ownership, but which link these issues more directly to intellectual property, expressive agency, and to speculation on the becoming-creative of AI.

[3]

(Dis)Locating Creativity, Agency, and Property in AI

When the American engineer and computer artist Michael A. Noll attempted to register his copyright in *Gaussian Quadratic* (1963), a software-generated plotter graphic that is now considered a foundational work of software-based generative art (fig. 2), he encountered difficulties linking questions of creative agency to questions of intellectual property (IP), in a prefiguration of similar issues that are now playing out in AI art contexts. Copyright registrars at the U.S. Library of Congress had concerns regarding the general eligibility of *Gaussian Quadratic* for such legal protection, and repeatedly denied Noll's request before it was finally granted.[1] *Gaussian Quadratic* had been created at Bell Labs, where Noll, who, throughout his career, has persistently resisted identification as an artist, was employed as an engineer and researcher (cf. Taylor 2014, 32ff.). As Noll (1994, 41) recalls,

1 Readers with specialist knowledge of copyright law may wonder if Noll was attempting to register the underlying software code as a literary work, or instead to register its outputs as individual artistic works. Unfortunately, Noll's (1994) own anecdotal retelling of the episode offers little clue, and no digital record of the copyright registration is available.

the work was initially deemed ineligible for copyright protection because the registrars viewed it as the creation of a computer system, rather than that of a human artist. This might seem like a progressive interpretation, but in a pragmatic sense it simply meant that from the copyright registrars' perspective, the law's requirement for an identifiable author/creator did not appear to be met. In response, Noll clarified that the graphic is, in fact, based on code written by a human, and explained that his program incorporates randomness to generate ever-different outputs. His second request was then also denied, this time based on the concern that even if a human author had been at work here, the randomness characterizing the work violated the "fixity" requirements of copyright law, i.e., the need for the work to exist in a fixed expression. Copyright protection for *Gaussian Quadratic* was finally granted when Noll rephrased his request a third time, insisting that even though the outputs of his generative algorithm are unpredictable, the human-authored code substrate represents an original and stable text, whose creativity is constituted precisely through its capacity to generate dynamic results.[2]

The contradictory chain of interpretations involved in the process of registering copyright in *Gaussian Quadratic* invokes the various kinds of speculation regarding non-human creative agency that I

2 Today, *Gaussian Quadratic* is considered as one of the first copyright-protected works of computer-generated art. Noll writes that AT&T and Bell Labs, his employers at the time, were hesitant to publicly support his creative activities. Indeed, permission for him and his collaborator Bela Julesz to claim intellectual property ownership in their work appears to have been granted in order to divert public attention away from the corporate entities themselves, perhaps on the assumption that the creative experiments would be of little commercial value, or even harmful to corporate image and strategy. It is worth mentioning that this general attitude would soon reverse, with prominent artist residency programs springing up at Bell Labs and many other IT corporations. A corollary of this development is that permission for participating artists to retain exclusive IP rights is now much less likely to be granted. On the emergence of artist residencies in corporate technology contexts, see Scarlett 2020.

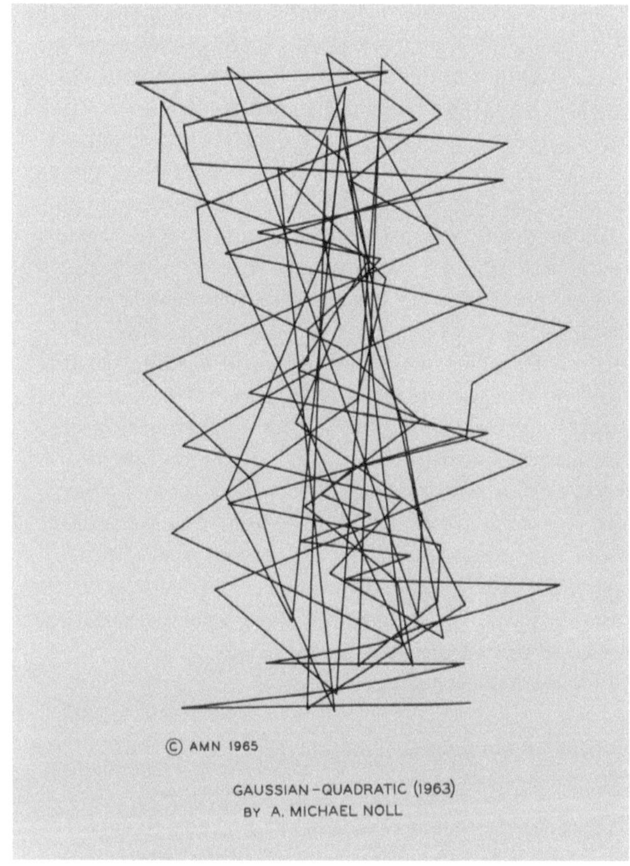

[Figure 2] Michael A. Noll, *Gaussian Quadratic* (1963). Copyright Victoria and Albert Museum; image used by permission.

have described in the previous chapter, and foreshadows how AI projects are now interfacing with similar questions of creativity, agency, and ownership. To me, the hesitations of the Library of Congress registrars indicate humanist and anthropocentric biases underlying their interpretation of Noll's work for the purpose of determining its eligibility for copyright protection. In this sense, the initial rejection of Noll's request suggests that the registrars may have humored, at least speculatively, the notion of a redistribution of creative agency from a human to a non-human entity; at the same time, the rejection shows that legally speaking, the registrars were unable to accept a computer as the artwork's author in the conventional sense. If the graphic was to be considered as the output of an autonomous computer, this meant that no valid author figure could be identified, and the graphic itself could not, consequence, be recognized as a copyright-protectable work of art. When Noll insisted that he himself was indeed the creator of the work, the Library of Congress registrars then questioned his creative agency, given that by his own admission he was not fully in control of his program's outputs. Ultimately, in order to be granted the protection that IP law commonly affords artists, Noll had to rescind on the main speculative implication enacted in this algorithm-driven generative work, namely that a shared creative agency existed between him and the technological system he used. (This implication resonates with the position of other early computer artists, including Frieder Nake, who similarly insisted that his work emerged from a collaborative working-together of human and computer.) From the perspective of the copyright registrars, *Gaussian Quadratic* could only exist as a copyright-protectable work of art if Noll asserted his authorial control over the generative system.

Compared to the complex and data-intensive computational tools available to contemporary artists working with AI today, the algorithm used to generate *Gaussian Quadratic* is quite straightforward. I would nevertheless argue that the work plays with the speculative possibilities of the posthumanist agential assemblage and its instantiation in computational functions, effects, technologies, or processes whose outcome can be interpreted as creative. Arguably, the copyright registrars acted in recognition of just such an interpretation when they initially rejected Noll's request. As such, the work highlights how, in an environment in which validation of a creative expression through IP mechanisms has become the norm, artistic experimentation with tools that are artificially intelligent (or interpreted as such) requires a rethinking of copyright issues in relation to agency and creativity.

Historically, the exclusive and exclusionary mechanisms through which agency and personhood have been granted (or withheld) have often served to disadvantage and exploit marginalized groups based on gender, race, ethnicity, sexual identity, political conviction, and other criteria. To dispute the agency of an individual, group, or community has often meant to withhold not only rights to personal freedom, self-determination, and freedom of expression, but also rights to own property. As discussed below, some humanist perspectives closely link agency and ownership, to the point of considering them as co-constitutive. In order to explore further how speculative figurations of agency in AI systems might disturb the aesthetic and socio-economic frameworks in which they are embedded, it is necessary to unpack how these frameworks themselves draw on anthropocentric conceptions of agency. This is my aim in the present chapter: to elaborate, based on underlying philosophical tenets and legal theory, conceptual links between agency, personhood, and ownership—first with a focus on how these links form a foundation of IP principles, and then in consideration of how such principles can (or cannot) be applied to AI. This paves the way for my discussion, in the subsequent chapters, of AI art projects that interfere drastically with contemporary ownership models.

AI Authorship According to Hegel

A good starting point is to explore links between legal concepts of property and philosophical conceptualizations of personality and personhood. I will do so by way of Hegel's personality theory (1821), which continues to serve as a significant reference point in explanatory and justificatory frameworks for private property. The theory assumes the following: unless a clear sense of self can be fixed in externalized manifestations, an individual cannot begin to know itself as such, cannot begin to fathom its own subjectivity, and as a consequence those around it will be unable to relate to it as an individual. When these externalized manifestations of self become an individual's property, the individual's legitimate ownership claims co-constitute its personality. Who would I be, in other words, without some kind of externalization of "me" that is expressed in material and/or immaterial constructs and artefacts over which I can assert control? This perspective thus posits property and personality as co-constitutive and inextricably linked. It underpins the anthropocentric ideal of the emergence of an autonomous agent that is philosophically, legally, socially, and economically recognized by its ability to own property.

As the legal philosopher Peter Drahos notes, property is so important in Hegel's concept of identity and personality because it is through its acquisition and management that the mind, in Hegelian terms a free and unbound entity, manages to "achieve [a] concrete form of existence in the world" (Drahos 1996, 76). This concrete form manifests as personality "through the appropriation of things" (ibid.), to which, Hegel writes, any individual should have an absolute right. Significantly, for Hegel it is not only material objects that are subject to such appropriation, nor are tangible artefacts the only medium in which the self can find expression. Rather, as Drahos observes, "mental aptitudes, erudition, [and] artistic skill" (77) play a similarly important role in Hegel's concept of the formation of personality. Once externalized in tangible form, these "inner possessions" therefore also render the individual as a person. The agency of an individual as constituted by its ownership of externalized artefacts thus hinges fundamentally on the "objectification" of the individual's will (cf. Palmer 2005, 139), or, in Hegelian terms, on the imposition of a concrete form ("occupancy") on an externality.

While some contemporary critical positions contest this Hegelian perspective, the logic of its compelling notion of authorship-as-ownership persists in IP theory and policy. Noll's *Gaussian Quadratic* is a case in point. The artist's difficulties in registering the work exemplify legal requirements according to which creative expressions need to be traceable to an originator; if these requirements are not satisfied, the aesthetic artefact is not eligible for copyright protection, and it becomes difficult for it to be owned, traded or gifted within the parameters that intellectual property law provides. If, in other words, no recognizable author of an aesthetic artefact work can be identified, then for many intents and purposes the artefact in question is no "work" at all. But if such an aesthetic artefact is indeed recognized as the original, creative expression of an identifiable author, this has significant implications for the nature and identity of this author figure.

A question raised by the copyright eligibility issues surrounding *Gaussian Quadratic* is what complications might arise when artificially intelligent agential assemblages become involved in creating (im)material artefacts which, following the Hegelian perspective, can be understood to engender personhood. What happens when such assemblages begin to operate autonomously, and detach from human subjectivity and knowability to such a degree that it is no longer possible to say, with any degree of authority, whether their outputs are "my" creations, and whether their decision-making processes and interpretations of information emerge from "my" thinking?

When non-human agential entities come into the picture, the anthropocentric logic underlying the Hegelian perspective—that personality forms through the externalization of will and the subsequent instantiation of this externalization as property—can be short-circuited. In such a situation, the "becoming-agent" through which, in a humanist framework, the individual is cast as creator and owner of things, is subject to various disturbances. What if, for example, an AI system is used in the making of an artwork in such a way that the human artist involved can no longer with certainty be considered as the creator of the work in question?

When Christie's promoted the auction sale of the AI-generated artwork *Portrait of Edmond Belamy* in October 2018 by invoking this suggestion, many observers argued that the sale could significantly disrupt the author- and ownership relations which conventionally structure the art world. While the work certainly raised a number of interesting questions, in the following chapter I will argue that the presumptive non-human creative agency manifest in *Portrait of Edmond Belamy* actually relies on strongly anthropocentric models of authorship, and ultimately perpetuates the ownership models the work was said to be disrupting. The example suggests, nevertheless, that the emergence of presumptively creative AI, even when it appears as part of agential assemblages that also include human artists, signals a potential decentering of human agency, and the destabilizing of the processes by which agency (and thus ownership) have been traditionally assigned and recognized.

If an AI system were to be accepted as creative in an anthropocentric sense of the term, what kind of status would it be assigned as it pushes beyond aesthetics and into the domains of ethics, law, and economy? Sketching out an answer to such a question requires a more detailed consideration of whether authorship/ownership claims could become vested in AI. As noted in the previous chapter, property is a fundamentally relational construct; it establishes and maintains relationships between owner and non-owners in respect of the owned property, and is demarcated by a clearly definable set of rights and responsibilities. But a property relation is also always dynamic, in the sense that at any given moment it is both fixed (i.e., property rights are clearly assigned and enforceable) and subject to change (i.e., property rights are generally alienable). Because property rights assume and/or assert the existence of an owner, they have conventionally relied on some concept of personhood through which the subject of the legal rights and duties linked to ownership can be defined. What is not always spelt out clearly, however, is whether the legal person thus constituted must in fact be a natural person. In a key essay on the subject, the legal theorist Margaret Radin has suggested that any entity can in theory hold property rights, as long as the law can recognize this entity as an owner (Radin 1982; for a critique of Radin's position, see Schnably 1993; an early exploration of these arguments in AI contexts can be found in Solum 1992). In practice, however, this recognition has long been tied to a *de facto* requirement that an owner must not only be a legal person but also human. There are, by now, a few contexts in which legal and economic theory have opened up traditional conceptualizations of personhood toward what might be described as a trans-human perspective on agency: non-human corporate entities, for example, are now recognized virtually everywhere as legal persons. AI, however, has for now not been afforded such a status. When it comes to intelligence and creativity, anthropocentric biases persist.

Legal theory generally links personhood to agency by way of the assumption that when an action occurs, it can be traced to an agent who has, presumptively, acted with intention. Hegel's personality theory illustrates how this perspective negotiates the line between philosophical perspectives on agency and legal theories of property; it also suggests that the conceptual foundations of intellectual property themselves express anthropocentric ideals of authorship and creativity (cf. Hughes 1988; Radin 1993; Schroeder 2006). The Hegelian perspective—"that the person becomes a real self only by engaging in a property relationship with something external" (Radin 1982, 972)—assumes both that an individual's personality is actualized externally through the institution of property, and that property functions as a prerequisite for the formation of an individual capable of recognizing itself and of being recognized as such by others (Hegel 1952, 42). When this logic is extended to AI, and when artificially intelligent technological systems are interpreted as exhibiting creative agency comparable to that of human agents, AI inevitably begins to undermine anthropocentric IP models.

Because the Hegelian perspective relies on principles of individual personhood and self-ownership, it is possible to derive from it the assumption that both the creator of an IP artefact and its owner must be natural persons (cf. Hughes 1988). In digital contexts, such an assumption can become grounds for the argument that AI, because it cannot qualify for "natural person" status, cannot author artworks, nor hold property rights in its expressions. With regard to agency, a similar logic can be applied: considering the personhood status that is required so that individuals can be recognized as authors, the agency that enables an individual to own property rights becomes linked to the agency that enables persons to express themselves creatively. As a consequence, copyright law has tended to assign ownership rights over any given creative expression to its presumptively human creators. The *U.S. Compendium of Copyright Practices* spells this out explicitly: "The U.S. Copyright Office will register an original work of authorship, provided that the work was created by a human being" (§306). But this formulation is open to challenges in contexts where it is unclear whether the human agent involved in the expressive act can, indeed, be meaningfully acknowledged as the creator. A good example is *Naruto v. Slater* (2018), a legal dispute in which People for Ethical Treatment of Animals (PETA) accused a photographer of copyright infringement, suing him on behalf of a monkey that had used the photographer's unattended camera for a series of now-famous "monkey selfies" (see Jiang 2019).

Can IP Law Accommodate Artistic AI?

I have already suggested that to speculate on the creativity of AI means inevitably also to speculate on AI agency, and thus to contend with the possibility of authorship and ownership rights vested in AI. Without a certain kind of creative agency, one cannot create; without a certain kind of legal agency, one cannot own. But if the U.S. Library of Congress' copyright registrars found it difficult to determine the legal status of a relatively simple generative graphic such as Noll's *Gaussian Quadratic*, then it is clear that advanced AI raises the stakes significantly. Yet, as the law and technology scholar James Grimmelmann notes, in many legal systems copyright law appears to have concluded, at least for the moment, "that it is for humans only" (Grimmelmann 2016).

The history of legal philosophy indicates that in addressing questions of legal personhood, law has typically either ignored the biological status of its subjects or has been ignorant of it (cf. Chopra and White 2011, 153). Considering this lack of clear direction regarding requirements for a legal subject to be human, the law and technology scholar Robert van den Hoven van Genderen suggests that any non-human person could theoretically be "in an equal position as an individual and natural person, unless otherwise provided by law" (van den Hoven van Genderen 2018, 30, referencing Naffine 2003). Concerning the legal concept of personhood, van den Hoven van Genderen summarizes three noteworthy perspectives: 1) "personhood means nothing more than the formal capacity to be a carrier of legal rights and duties;" 2) "a (legal) person is any reasonable human creature;" 3) a person is a "rational, responsible actor." Only the first and the third of these definitions can potentially be extended to AI; the third, additionally, has the potential to exclude some human agents (ibid., 35ff.). The question, then, is whether these perspectives can be linked to the kind of agency implied by the broader concept of authorship, which is being ever more closely approximated by expressive AI assemblages that might involve human participants, software, hardware, and algorithmic operations alongside one another, in enacting what I have described as a relational, multi-modal kind of posthumanist creative agency in the previous chapter.

But debates concerning new ontologies of authorship that branch off from existing paradigms remain strongly marked by anthropocentric bias. Here, once again, AI-generated outputs tend to be compared to human-made expressions, which can result in some rather strange logic. The legal scholars

Yanisfky-Ravid and Velez-Hernandez (2018), for example, suggest that many works produced by what they call creative robots would surely be copyrightable—if only they had been created by humans. This perspective may seem like a challenge to the above-cited sentiment that copyright is "for humans only," but it also assumes that machine creativity is, essentially, like human creativity. The authors' suggestion to extend copyright eligibility to machine-made artworks thus hinges on a self-contradictory anthropomorphization of expressive AI, robots, and other non-human entities as human-like.

Oliver Bown, a researcher in the field of computational creativity, is among many who have voiced concerns regarding such a perspective, by pointing out that if the possibility of non-human creative agency is taken seriously, it must be accepted that machine-creativity might not function "in particularly human-like ways" (2015, 18). It might instead match what Ray Kurzweil and others (Kurzweil 2005; Bridle 2018) have invoked as the specter of fundamentally unknowable non-human intelligence. Thus returns the underlying issue of whether or not creativity itself is a fundamentally human quality. In the editorial introduction to a topical special issue of *Philosophy & Technology*, David Gunkel observes that "the one remaining bulwark of human exceptionalism appears to be creativity and artistry" (2017, 263). As Gunkel himself notes, this opinion of course does not stand unchallenged, and some might argue that invocations of such exceptionalism are, in fact, at the core of the anthropomorphizing rhetoric that is often applied to AI. If creativity is truly unique to humans, then any admission that AI could also act creatively is either a radical rethinking of "the human," or already an anthropomorphization of artificial intelligence. Accordingly, machine-generated artworks can help at least to "stress-test" (264) prevalent assumptions, definitions, and categories concerning what it means to be human (or not), what it means to have creative agency (or not), and how to disentangle complications regarding the anthropomorphization of AI.

A recent essay by the legal scholars Carys Craig and the late Ian Kerr offers one of the most comprehensive critiques to date of the anthropomorphizing tendencies with which emerging AI technologies are sometimes approached (Craig and Kerr, 2021). Writing from an interdisciplinary perspective, the authors adopt Kate Darling's HCI/HRI concept of "anthropomorphic framing," which describes tendencies to conceive of AI functionality and "behavior" in human terms—for example by giving robot humanoid shapes, by naming AI systems, or by using anthropocentric terminology to describe AI activities (Darling 2017, cited in Craig and Kerr, 32).[3] As Craig and Kerr show, much of the discourse that links artificial intelligence to creative expression works not only by way of anthropomorphizing AI, but also, importantly, by way of an elaborate replaying of the myth of the romantic author figure. In other words, one of the most powerful ways of positing AI as "author" is to attach to it romantic notions of creativity, such as the fictions of *ex nihilo* creation and of the unified, singular author figure. This approach is exemplified by Arthur I. Miller's (2019) recent book-length survey of AI art: the book is an impressively comprehensive endeavor, but its notion of creativity is predominantly derived from human "genius" figures, whose superior brains serve as the models to which the presumptive creativity of computer "brains" is compared. Here, an oddly inverted mirror image of the idea of creativity's "effective computability" (see chapter 1) emerges, in the form of Miller's insistence on the all-too human(ist) nature of genius.

A reliance on humanist ideals that have traditionally framed definitions of human creativity may be helpful for arguing that AI is capable of acting independently in producing expressions that satisfy the cognitive scientist Margaret Boden's widely used creativity criteria of novelty, originality, and unexpectedness

3 While my discussion adopts this concept, I use the phrase "anthropocentric framing" instead, to reflect the fact that my focus is less on the anthropomorphization of AI than it is on tendencies to design and interpret AI functionality from anthropocentric viewpoints.

(1990). But just like the traditional models on which such a perspective draws, this line of argumentation will likely ignore the dialogic and relational processes that ultimately constitute human authorship. In other words, such a view on AI creativity perpetuates assumptions regarding the exceptional uniqueness and supremacy of the humanist, individualized subject that post-anthropocentric, posthumanist critical thinking wishes to critique. A conclusion to be drawn from Craig and Kerr's insightful discussion is thus that even when the idea of AI creativity is proposed as a radical counterpoint or extension to human creative agency, at its heart this often represents a particularly problematic type of anthropocentric framing.

To approach AI creativity through an anthropocentric lens is to keep creative expression at a remove from its relational, social, communicative, and collaborative aspects, which are also ignored in the romantic rhetoric of original genius, and which are, for the most part, incompatible with the narrowly conceived perspective of IP law. In this way, an idealized concept of the singular creative spirit that has served to underpin the propertization of creative expression is reproduced in many perspectives on AI creativity and AI authorship. This is precisely how Miller's survey of AI art proceeds, and it is not surprising that the author's anthropocentric bias prevents him from imagining anything radically new or different in AI art. In Miller's account, the human geniuses that form the basis for his definition of creativity delineate a genealogy that is almost exclusively male, white, and occidental. Much like a dataset with poorly labelled contents, Miller's discussion therefore reproduces the biases inscribed in longstanding fantasies of creative genius and singular authorship, which feminist theorists of law and culture including Rosemary C. Coombe, Ann Bartow, Carys Craig, and many others, have long criticized as a gendered, patriarchal, and elitist subject position (e.g., Coombe 1994, 1998; Bartow 2006; Craig 2015). Regardless of the angle from which issues of AI creativity, AI authorship and AI agency are approached, for now the majority of legal scholarship on the subject seems to arrive at one of two conclusions. The first is that because AI cannot technically claim a capability for authoring creative expressions, it does not have agency. The second inverts this logic, to suggest that because AI cannot technically be assigned agency, it cannot therefore be meaningfully understood as capable of authoring creative expressions. Both perspectives are impaired by the same central fallacy of imagining AI creativity in anthropocentric terms, and the assumption that the creative abilities of AI simply do not resemble those of human agents enough to warrant the legal recognition of AI systems as potential authors.

As van den Hoven van Genderen (2018) and others have noted, in most legal systems the concept of personhood is much more flexible than the concept of copyright. Specifically, while broader legal theories of personhood tend not to specify that the person under consideration must be a human agent, copyright statutes often do include such a requirement.[4] Unsurprisingly, these discrepancies themselves are likely to generate considerable debate both in favor and against the idea of formally extending the kind of agency required for authorship to AI. Pamela Samuelson, a key theorist of IP issues in relation to emerging technologies, has addressed some of the challenges AI can pose in this context as early as 1985, but research continues to be mired in fundamental definitional disagreements. (A comprehensive survey of conflicting opinions is included in Guihot and Rimmer, 2019.)

The law and technology scholar Annemarie Bridy, for example, considers contemporary AI as "authors-in-fact" that simply cannot (yet) be recognized as "authors-in-law" (2016). Craig and Kerr conclude that AI is not currently capable of authorship

4 At the time of writing, Copyright Acts that cannot accommodate AI-generated works on the basis that they are not authored by human agents exist, for example, in the U.S., in Germany, in Australia, and in Japan; in the UK, copyright can be extended to AI-generated works, but the right is assigned to the human creator of the computational system (see Yamamoto 2018; UK Copyright, Designs and Patent Act, s.9(3)).

because AI cannot participate in the shared, dialogic, and socio-culturally embedded processes that characterize creativity; as they note, the anthropomorphic framing of AI merely "reinforce[s] the illusion that machines possess a kind of intelligence and expressive agency that they do not—and cannot—in fact have" (2021, 70). Similarly, Aaron Hertzmann, writing against the background of computer science and art history, argues that "art is something created by social agents, and so computers cannot be credited with authorship of art in our current understanding" (2018, 1). Grimmelmann, finally, notes that computers cannot currently be said to be capable of authoring anything at all because of the prevailing legal requirements, which leads him to propose that the designation of "computer-generated" (2016) works is overall more accurate. By contrast, an argument in favor of the (full or partial) extendibility of copyright to AI-generated works could be that the law's technical definitions are always intended to be inclusive. Originality and creativity thresholds prescribed by copyright statutes, for example, tend to be relatively easy to satisfy, and generally don't take into account aesthetic considerations. The evolving history of copyright law includes many precedents that point in this direction.[5]

A further relevant thread in research on this subject is that even if AI cannot be granted full authorship status, it must be acknowledged at least that AI "assists" human authors, a point already highlighted in Pamela Samuelson's (1985) early writing on the topic. This view lends itself to the suggestion that existing work-for-hire rules could be applied to AI outputs (e.g., Yanisky-Ravid and Velez-Hernandez 2017; Hristov 2017). The work-for-hire concept represents a contractual twist to traditional notions

5 The legal literature on this subject is vast. Relevant case law includes *Feist Publications, Inc v. Rural Telephone Service Co* [1991] USSC 50 (U.S. context); *Infopaq International A/A v Danske Dagblades Forening* [2009] ECJ 17 (EU context); *Telstra II* (Aus); *CCH Canadian Ltd. v Law Society of Upper Canada* [2004] SCC 13 (Canada). Legal theoretical scholarship on the topic includes, for example, Samuelson 1985; Farr 1989; Bridy 2012; or Yu 2017.

of authorship: it categorizes creators as workers laboring under contract, whose IP rights are relegated to the human or corporate entities in whose employment they are. In human contexts, this type of arrangement applies to a growing majority of practitioners in the so-called creative industries, and has been theorized as an exploitative construct that undermines human agency and ownership rights (see, for example, Hesmondalgh 2012). When this concept is transferred to AI contexts, anthropocentric bias again becomes apparent: the idea of applying work-for-hire rules to AI requires that AI entities are implicitly viewed as authors before their creators' rights can be relegated to those owning or controlling the AI system. AI, in this scenario, would have to be understood as laboring for human agents, which also means that critiques concerning the exploitation of human creative labor in work-for-hire schemes could be extended to the labor presumptively exerted by AI. For the moment, such concerns would be counteracted, for example, in the argument that AI-as-instrument merely assists human creativity and/or labor as a kind of tool (see, for example, Steinert 2017; Hertzmann 2018), or that it represents, at best, a "medium" of expression (Mazzone and Elgammal 2019).

My survey of how questions concerning creative agency play out at the intersection of law and AI is far from comprehensive. It shows, nevertheless, that there is no agreement, among legal theorists, law makers, and policy advisors, on how best to go about acknowledging, disavowing, or plainly ignoring the speculative emergence of AI agency along with all of its critical implications. Diverging perspectives, often revolving around more practical concerns, continue to evolve. The Australian Copyright Act, for instance, bases its requirement that any author must be a human agent not on philosophical, aesthetic, or ethical concerns, but on much more pragmatic reasoning: the argument here is that because copyright in a work is designed to expire a certain number of years after its author's death, a machinic non-human agent cannot be recognized as an "author"

[4]

Copies Without Originals? AI-Generated Artworks and All-Too-Human Ownership Claims

The posthumanist agential assemblage raises difficult questions concerning the speculative possibility of non-human creativity. In particular, it can disturb intellectual property (IP) models that presuppose identifiable human creators as the originators and owners of creative expressions. As I argued in the preceding chapter, what complicates this discussion is that the concepts of creativity and authorship themselves are often framed anthropocentrically. Anthropomorphizing and anthropocentrically biased rhetoric also persists in digital art. One consequence is that some of the new issues AI art provokes regarding questions of authorship, provenance, and IP end up playing out along familiar vectors of all-too human ownership disputes. In this chapter, the first major auction sale of an AI-generated work of art serves as an example of how AI art can end up reproducing strategic frameworks of AI instrumentalization, and thereby close off speculative posthumanist horizons of non-human agency embodied in or enacted through AI.

In October 2018, the canvas-based, AI-generated work titled *Portrait of Edmond Belamy* (2018) was sold for the record-setting price of US$432,500 at a well-publicized auction at Christie's. Judging by commentary from art critics and the mainstream press, the event appeared to suggest that an existential identity crisis was unfolding in the world of contemporary art (see Shaw 2018; Saltz 2018; Pepi 2018). Produced by the French Obvious Collective, *Portrait of Edmond Belamy* was generated using a Generative Adversarial Network (GAN), a type of machine learning technology increasingly popular among digital artists. Mounted in a gilt-edged frame, the square canvas of *Portrait of Edmond Belamy* depicts the eerily diffuse portrait of a male figure and features tonal and compositional details reminiscent of classic portraiture, with perhaps a hint of Francis Bacon's iconic style (fig. 3). Significantly, the information panel displayed next to the work at the auction preview did not give an artist name. Instead, the piece was described as being "not the product of a human mind" but "a work of art created by an algorithm" (Christie's 2018).

Christie's claim drew significant attention in the popular press, particularly since the work was to be sold alongside high-priced artworks whose creators fit very neatly with humanist notions of the genius artist figure. The suggestion that no such figure had been involved in creating *Portrait of Edmond Belamy* caused a stir in the high-end art market, where the commercial value of artworks is generally tied not only to aesthetic value and considerations of artistic mastery, nor only to a work's uniqueness or scarcity, but also to the personage and pedigree of its creator(s). Artists and theorists alike have worked to disrupt humanist conceptions of the artist figure over the course of the past century or so; but in the institutional, commercial, and critical mainstreams of the art world, "the artist" tends to persist in the figuration of the singular, unified, individualized creative spirit embodied in a human agent. As I have suggested in the previous chapter, the importance of this figure persists also because without it, an artwork cannot easily enjoy the protections conventionally offered by IP legislation, and it may consequently be difficult to attach a stable monetary value to such a work.

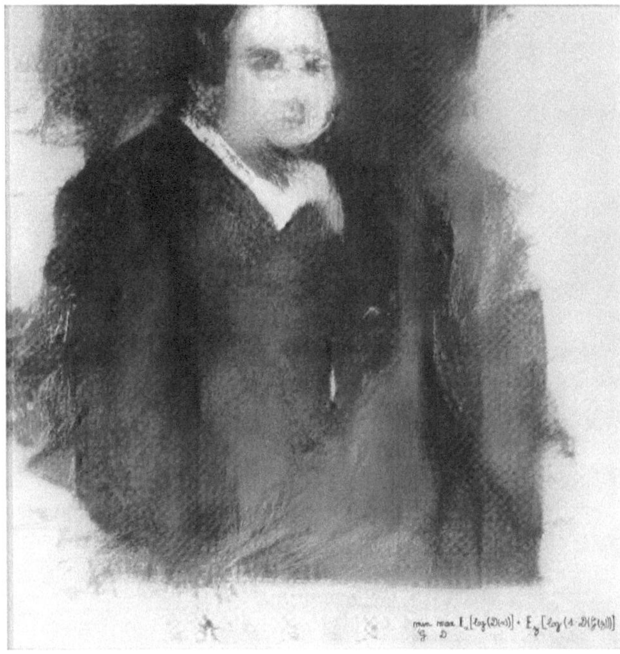

[Figure 3] Obvious Collective, *Portrait of Edmond Belamy* (2018). Public domain image source: Wikimedia Foundation.

The romantic fiction of the author figure serves well to uphold efforts to link scarcity to aesthetic value, and furthermore to pinpoint the "natural" owner of any given aesthetic artefact. This ideal also continues to be cultivated in the institutionalized art world, where all kinds of stakeholders, from commercial galleries and art fairs to museums, private collections, and art critics assign aesthetic value by invoking principles that align closely with IP's core mechanisms for identifying and controlling monetary value bound in creative expressions. It is hardly an exaggeration to suggest that in certain contexts, an artwork to which no creator can be attributed is undesirable because it cannot easily be captured by the frameworks through which value would conventionally be attached to it. In this sense, the excitement and anxiety inspired by the auctioning of *Portrait of Edmond Belamy* expressed a concern that if a clearly identifiable (human) author figure could indeed be supplanted by a new type of non-human creative agency, or perhaps even by an agential assemblage that lacks an identifiable center, the value propositions that buoy the art world would be radically undermined.

The excitement in the lead-up to the auctioning of *Portrait of Edmond Belamy* conveyed several concerns: if the embodiment of value in artworks relies on the principle of scarcity and the esteem of a clearly identifiable artist figure, then any work that can be meaningfully interpreted as having been autonomously created by a non-human entity must cause a significant disturbance. Without an identifiable author, and perhaps also eluding legal definitions of the "work" as such, such an aesthetic artefact might become unownable, in the sense that no stable value could be fixed to it. The auctioning of *Portrait of Edmond Belamy* was therefore a risky (or at least provocative) undertaking. Christie's aim was, of course, to demonstrate that a high commercial value can very well be attached to a computer-generated, presumptively authorless aesthetic artefact. But in doing so, Christie's was also contributing to a development that could pose a potential threat to the art market's viability: if an artwork created by an algorithm could be sold for a substantial amount of money, might this not suggest that authorial mastery and pedigree are not, after all, supreme tools for controlling an artwork's aesthetic-*qua*-monetary value?

By the time *Portrait of Edmond Belamy* achieved its astonishing sale price of more than forty times of the estimate, the excitement surrounding the work had somewhat shifted in focus. The work, intended to model a new form of non-human creativity, was now also the subject of a much more conventional controversy that replayed familiar human-centered authorship disputes. As it turned out, the members of Obvious

Collective, despite taking credit for the design of the AI system that generated *Portrait of Edmond Belamy*, had in fact appropriated much of the code substrate for the work from the young American AI artist Robbie Barrat.[1] *Portrait of Edmond Belamy* thus offers a good context not merely for asking how AI art might challenge existing perspectives on creative agency, authorship, and ownership, but also how the intention to do so can misfire, and end up achieving little more than putting a twist on anthropocentrically framed authorship disputes.

Some art market stakeholders and the mainstream press were keen to celebrate the sale of *Portrait of Edmond Belamy* as proof that AI-based machine creativity is not only possible, but has already become a reality. From this perspective, the high auction price was understood to have reified the portrait as a valuable artwork, perhaps much more reliably than any art critic could have done. AI theorists, AI developers, and digital artists offered less favorable responses, and argued instead that AI creativity in the anthropocentric sense remains impossible, that *Portrait of Edmond Belamy* is conceptually and technically shallow, and that established norms of cultural ownership would not be fundamentally shaken by AI-generated aesthetic artefacts. Importantly, this criticism also highlighted the extent to which Obvious Collective relied on the unacknowledged reusing of the work of another (human) artist (see Vincent 2018).

The controversy surrounding the collective's appropriation of Robbie Barrat's code and data inflects the claims concerning the

1 Readers will have noticed that the images on the book cover bear a striking similarity to *Portrait of Edmond Belamy*. The images were created by the Australian AI artist and researcher Tom White, in an effort to test the claim that Obvious Collective had indeed copied Robbie Barrat's work (see Artnome 2018 for a Twitter thread debating the similarities and implications). Using the underlying code shared by Barrat on Github, the results achieved by White suggest that Obvious Collective may well have worked with Barrat's code. In the spirit of transparency, White also published a software repository elucidating his process as well as his use of Barrat's original model (White n.d.).

non-human origin of *Portrait of Edmond Belamy* in fascinating ways. For context: Barrat (n.d.) had freely shared the code-base used for his own work on the online repository and collaboration tool GitHub, used by many programmers for sharing software code. Based on Barrat's use of Creative Commons copyright licenses, the collective's use of his material was, in legal terms, permissible. The "misappropriation" under discussion here is thus primarily ethical in nature, rather than a by-the-books violation of IP rights; accordingly, the issue was never addressed in court, but rather in the online tribunals of Twitter feeds and Reddit threads, where violations of informal cultural ownership norms are frequently deliberated (see Zeilinger 2012). Nevertheless, Barrat's (2018) complaint and the attention it garnered mark a shift from the lofty speculative-philosophical heights of "creative AI" toward more familiar grounds of anthropocentric IP ownership issues. Here, the central question is no longer just whether the machine learning system that had generated the portrait should be considered a creative/artistic entity, but also how the dispute between Barrat and the Obvious collective is impacted by claims concerning the AI origins of *Portrait of Edmond Belamy*. In other words, what is at stake here is the question of how to culturally and legally negotiate ownership disputes in instances where non-human entities become involved in creative processes.

GAN "Creativity"

For the creation of *Portrait of Edmond Belamy*, the Obvious collective relied on GAN-based machine learning technology, which has become a favored tool among AI artists working with image synthesis (see also Zeilinger 2021). GAN—Generative Adversarial Network—refers to a type of artificial neural network that can be trained to generate novel content on the basis of training processes that rely on large datasets of pre-existing materials. The technology has become relatively accessible in recent years, and part of what makes it so attractive to digital artists is that its outputs are curiously balanced between predictability and unexpectedness. Because GAN outputs can satisfy requirements featuring in widely accepted definitions of creativity and originality (e.g., Boden 1990), GANs have become a playground for much artistic speculation on AI creativity.

In-depth technical explanations of the technology have become widely available, along with step-by-step tutorials to guide users through the setup of GAN systems trained on openly accessible datasets. A more detailed description is nevertheless useful here, as it allows me to demonstrate how, beyond anthropocentric analogies between human and computational creativity, GAN technology undermines the integrity of the unified, singular artist/author figure even while it appears to emulate it. GAN technology is thus best understood as aligned with a progressive posthumanist notion of expressive agency, learning, and creative expression. This contradicts romantic ideals of creativity and originality, and resonates with the tactical potentials of AI as introduced earlier.

Conventionally, GAN systems consist of at least two discrete computational neural networks that are described as "Generator" and "Discriminator." In the iterative training processes that characterize GANs, these discrete units are understood to function as "adversaries"—one produces outputs, the other compares them to a training dataset and validates or rejects them. To train the system (or for the system to be able to "learn"), a dataset of appropriate example images is assembled, most commonly based on readily available collections or by using scraper tools that collect relevant images online. The Generator network will then begin to produce image outputs until the set goal, that is, a novel image that satisfies certain criteria (often with a focus on similarity to the training set, i.e., perceived "authenticity") is reached. Importantly, the Generator does not have access to the dataset of pre-existing images; it begins its image-creation process without "knowledge" of what the desired output should look like, and relies on the Discriminator network for feedback.

With no information to go on, it can be expected that the Generator's first image output will consist of randomly placed pixels, which will then be passed to the Discriminator network for validation. In contrast to the Generator, the Discriminator has access to the training dataset of pre-existing images, against which each of the Generator's image outputs is now compared. When the Discriminator rejects an output, this evaluation is communicated back to the Generator. Depending on the configuration of the system, the feedback may consist of a simple binary response, but it might also include additional information, for example regarding the accuracy of color content or compositional details. The Generator now compares the feedback received with information concerning its previous outputs, adjusts its rendering algorithms, and iterates its next output, which is again passed for evaluation to the Discriminator. And so on.

Over a large number of iterations, which can reach into hundreds of thousands of repetition-and-difference cycles, the Generator "learns" from its mistakes and improves its outputs, which will begin to match the training data more and more closely until a threshold of accuracy is reached, beyond which the Discriminator is no longer able to distinguish the Generator outputs from the "real" contents of the training dataset. At some point, the GAN system as a whole could thus be understood to have successfully "learned" to produce, with a constant and predictable success rate, images that sit above the threshold of what can be meaningfully interpreted, both by the Discriminator and by human observers, as part of the image set that makes up the training data. To generate a complex image such as the semi-realistic portrait of a human figure depicted in *Portrait of Edmond Belamy*, the Discriminator network will require access to a relevant training dataset of existing portraits. Portraiture, of course, has long been a key area of artistic production and art historical scholarship, so that useful training data is relatively easy to assemble.[2]

Significantly, in lay descriptions of GAN functionality the iterative back-and-forth between Generator and Discriminator is often characterized as a competition, a kind of cat-and-mouse game in which the Generator attempts to convince the Discriminator that its outputs are "real." In the context of artistic outputs, this logic would characterize the Generator as a kind of art forger trying to trick a master artist into accepting a masterfully executed copy as a genuine original, and to misinterpret "fake" as "real," or "copy" as "original" (see Zeilinger 2021 for a more detailed analysis of this terminology). This invokes Lev Manovich's "AI art Turing test," (2019): in Manovich's test scenario, the "creativity" of an AI system is meant to be determined by its ability to fool a human art critic into erroneously believing that the output under consideration was created by a human artist. As discussed in chapter 2, an immediate issue with this approach is that it conceptualizes creativity and artfulness in fundamentally anthropocentric terms, in the sense that the threshold for AI creativity is here understood as its ability to successfully pass itself off as human creativity. Nevertheless, what can be usefully derived from Manovich's version of the Turing test is that an expressive machine learning system such as a GAN is, in essence, a new type of highly sophisticated copy machine. Importantly, this perspective reveals itself as both correct and misleading. Strictly speaking, the Generator's outputs can never constitute copies or reproductions of anything at all, since the system does not have the kind of direct access to source materials that is implied by the anthropocentric analogies of the forger, copyist, or apprentice imitator. However, while the Generator, in other words, cannot be said to copy the training data in any conventionally meaningful sense of the term, a GAN system's conjuring up of romantic ideals

2 Many lists of relevant open datasets can be found online (e.g., ArtNome, n.d.; Coding Dürer, n.d.; and Berkley Library, n.d.).

of creativity and artistic expression also disturbs these same ideals.

Despite the nominally adversarial nature of the interaction between Generator and Discriminator, the two discrete units work in tandem to form what can be described as a sophisticated appropriation machine, capable of approximating style, content, and other desired qualities of the training materials without directly copying these source materials. Conceptually, it is thanks to this capability that GANs bear resemblance to the creative minds of human agents: not in the traditional sense of the spirited original genius figure who produces unique creative works, but rather in a more progressive sense of creativity as a fundamentally relational, embedded, and dialogic process. To turn things on their head a bit, following this logic it is entirely feasible not only to describe computational creativity with reference to the way humans learn, but also to describe human creativity by borrowing from the conceptual register of machine learning: in such a formulation, creativity becomes the ability to generate novel content by iterating derivative approximations of pre-existing materials, to the point where imitation, astonishingly, dissolves into unexpected outputs that can pass as original and, potentially, as creative.

Clearly, this observation stands in stark contradiction to traditional ideals of artistic genius. It resonates, instead, with the more progressive view that influence, imitation, mimicry, and copying form the core of how human agents acquire language, learn a craft, and, indeed, create art (see Boon 2010 for an elaborate rethinking of creativity and originality in relation to copying practices). In this sense, it would be wrong to entirely reject analogies between GAN-style machine learning and human creativity. We should hold on to this analogy at least because it does a good job of undermining the notion of the romantic (human-only) artist figure who creates from *tabula rasa*. In other words, to acknowledge the dialogic interactions between Generator and Discriminator (or even entanglements between

Generator, Discriminator, training data, and human "curator") is a good way of re-emphasizing the relational dimensions of human creativity itself.

This means that GAN-based generative tools and their outputs can serve to inscribe the operational logic of machine learning with a notion of creative expression that challenges perspectives of the centrality and supremacy of the unified, singular, and spirited human artist, and their unique ability to create original expressions. A GAN-based AI art practice that engages with agency and ownership issues tactically mobilizes the complicated entanglements of Generator and Discriminator with the corpus of training materials in order to link the operational logic of GAN systems with a progressive notion of creative expression that approximates the posthumanist perspectives introduced earlier. I will return to this point in my concluding chapter, where I discuss GANs as "generative adversarial copy machines" that are inherently incompatible with any rhetoric framing of creative AI that relies on traditional, anthropocentric notions of creativity.

"What matter who's speaking"

Portrait of Edmond Belamy fails to mobilize these critical aspects of GAN technology, and instead attempts to sketch out a much more traditional kind of author figure. The complexities of GAN functionality, and its critical implications for how creativity as such might be rethought in AI contexts, do not figure into this narrative. In fact, the stories told by Christie's and Obvious Collective to position *Portrait of Edmond Belamy* as a creative expression produced autonomously by an AI system resolve into stark contradictions that emphasize, rather than erase, the work's anthropocentric framing.

When Robbie Barrat asserted his authorship of the code base used for creating *Portrait of Edmond Belamy* and challenged Obvious Collective regarding their appropriation of his code and data, he fundamentally questioned the idea that the work had been "created by an algorithm" (Christie's 2018). Instead, he argued, human agents had very clearly (and inevitably) intervened at every stage of the algorithmic and technical process of generating the work in question. In the case of a GAN-generated image like the one under discussion here, a number of such human interventions can be easily identified. For example, one or more human agents will inevitably be involved in the processes of: 1) designing and setting up the machine learning network used; 2) compiling and/or labelling the data on which the system is trained; 3) deciding the criteria for "successful" outputs; 4) monitoring outputs and making determinations regarding the continuation/termination of the iterative learning/output process; and 5) curating the resulting outputs. A similar spectrum of human involvement in the facilitation of AI outputs has been noted by various researchers, and also by Robbie Barrat himself (cf. Manovich 2019, 5; Elgammal et al. 2018, 2; Bailey 2018). These observations may appear quite self-evident, but they help to foreground the human stakes in GAN-based AI art, thereby complicating the picture of presumptive AI creativity. As noted, this does not mean that the notion of such creativity should be disavowed, but rather that AI art enacts new kinds of entanglements between human and non-human agential entities (or, indeed, between non-human entities, such as the Generator and Discriminator components of a GAN system). This perspective is entirely ignored, however, in how Christie's and Obvious sought to frame *Portrait of Edmond Belamy*.

Two specific aspects of the work are noteworthy in this context. The first one involves a peculiar numerical cipher found on the canvas, which was included in place of an artist's signature to underpin the conceit that the work had been authored by an AI system (the signature can be seen in fig. 3). Christie's (2018) promotional material interpreted this as an indication that Obvious Collective had ceded authorial claims to the AI system. But by which convention does the quasi-authorial inscription of an algorithmic cipher-signature here signal the existence of (or, literally, the production of) a non-human author figure to whom the work could be attributed? As an index of the presence of creative AI, this suggestion is immediately undermined by the anthropomorphizing nature of the gesture itself: to sign a work of art is the supreme signal of human authorship. The gesture is also closely linked to the ownership models that have developed around the notion that authors should be entitled to the expressions in which their creative labor is inscribed. In the given context, the cipher-signature is thus ultimately self-contradictory: on the one hand, it is meant to suggest that the computational entity responsible for the creation of *Portrait of Edmond Belamy* is "like" a human agent; on the other hand, the manifestation of the signature in algorithmic form is interpreted as an assertion that this agency is, precisely, not human. I would argue, on this point, that a signature is a particularly unsuitable way of signaling a shift of creative agency from the human to the non-human.

The second issue is that in addition to having appropriated the code base for the work from Robbie Barrat (a human author-specter who, despite the initial lack of attribution, will forever haunt this AI-generated artwork), Obvious Collective also draw attention to a further author figure. As the members of the collective have themselves stated, the algorithm that is partially reproduced in the image was authored not by themselves nor by Barrat, but by Ian Goodfellow, a key developer in the AI community whose contribution the collective wished to honor. With this background information, the partial inclusion of the algorithm on the canvas gains additional significance—not as an authorial index asserting provenance or authenticity as a work of art created by a non-human entity, but instead as a reference or citation. Goodfellow is widely credited for the invention of GAN-type machine learning (Goodfellow et al. 2014). The achievement has earned him the nickname of "GANfather," a designation that invokes godfather-like powers of patriarchal-*qua*-authorial control, and which suggests quite the opposite of a relegation of creative agency to a non-human entity. To round out this broken chain of quasi-authorial gestures, Ian Goodfellow is also explicitly referenced in the title of the work itself: "Belamy" is a Frenchified version of the GANfather's last name, and thus yet another way for the collective to inadvertently draw *Portrait of Edmond Belamy* into a complex network of human and non-human collaborations. Ultimately, the collective's citation-as-signature undermines the proposition that the technology used is capable of independent, autonomous creative expression. This highlights—but does not acknowledge—the relational qualities of the creative processes that made the output possible.

How, then, should the processes involved in the production of *Portrait of Edmond Belamy* be characterized? Following the arguments I have developed here, it would be wrong to recognize Obvious Collective as the creators of the work; but neither can its members be considered as stewards or facilitators of a new form of non-human creative agency. Furthermore, even though the GAN system used by the collective draws on code and training data authored by others, it is also incorrect to call them plagiarists, since the system rendered an output that fits many definitions of originality and novelty, and which, in any case, hovers outside the bubble of IP and authorial influence as it is conventionally understood. In my view, the most interesting characterization of the collective would be one that perceives its members as participants in a new form of agential assemblage; unfortunately, this is not a role that the members of the collective have embraced. Instead, the speculative relegation of creative agency to AI by way of the various flourishes injected into *Portrait of Edmond Belamy* reveals itself as human-made artifice, of a sort that was perhaps felt to be necessary in order to render "creative AI" credible in the mainstream, property-oriented context for which the work was produced.

There is, I would argue, an additional reading of the presumptively non-human creative agency that is manifest in this work: I view Christie's anthropocentric framing of creative AI as an implicit assurance that a paradigmatic change in technology-based creative expression (such as it might be constituted by the emergence of creative AI) need not disrupt existing practices of tying an artwork's value to a clearly determinable, singular author figure. This, of course, also doubles as an assurance that AI art will not disrupt, but rather extend the value propositions of the art market. If a new form of AI-based, non-human expressive agency could channel value into an aesthetic artefact while remaining under the control of an underlying human proprietor, IP claims in the resulting work could be easily managed in familiar ways, and such an "authorless" work of AI art could become a highly desirable commodity indeed. Perhaps, this is precisely what the high sales price achieved in the auction indicates.

In this reading, the way in which *Portrait of Edmond Belamy* mobilizes AI technology reveals itself as strategic—rather than tactical—in nature. Despite surface appearances, and despite the rhetoric framing of the work, the specter of creative AI is here posited as something that remains intimately tied to humanist concepts of creative expression, authorship, and the markets they serve. In other words, *Portrait of Edmond Belamy* speculates on non-human expressive agency for the purpose of reasserting quite conventional notions of creativity, and it does so by drawing on an authorship concept that perpetuates the cultural logic of IP. Nothing about this logic is challenged, let alone changed, by the way in which *Portrait of Edmond Belamy* attempts to transpose a conventional authorship concept into a non-human context. Put differently, the work does not extend Foucault's notion of the "author function" (1980) forward into a posthumanist context of generative AI, where the unifying functions of traditional authorship could be reconfigured, or potentially dissolved. Rather, the work is oriented toward reproducing, in the context of presumptively non-human creative expression, a romantic notion of authorship that continues to serve as a "privileged moment of individualization," as Foucault famously put it, in a way that remains highly useful for IP's anthropocentric enclosures of creative expression.

The narrative surrounding the work and its auction sale sought to position *Portrait of Edmond Belamy* as indicative of AI's ability to express itself creatively without relying on human computer artists. But Obvious Collective's implementation of this suggestion appears clumsy and ultimately self-defeating. Given the highly conventional nature of the AI author figure that is proposed here, in concluding I would argue that if *Portrait of Edmond Belamy* is to be understood as putting forward any radical proposition at all, then this has nothing to do with the speculative emergence of posthumanist AI creativity. Rather, the proposition here appears to be that a viable market for digital art that can pretend to not rely on human artists is indeed possible, and already emerging. *Portrait of Edmond Belamy* does not gesture toward a decentering of human agency in an aesthetic or socio-cultural sense, nor to any political implications of such a move, but instead toward a reinscription of anthropocentric ownership models in AI art contexts. The story told by Obvious Collective and Christie's concerning a speculative decentering of human agency enacted through *Portrait of Edmond Belamy* does not proceed along tactical vectors that might disturb IP. Instead, the work represents a strategic effort to transpose a humanist ideal of authorship into an AI context, such that the art market's existing value propositions can continue to function.

[5]

AI Art and the Deniability of Human Creative Agency

In the previous chapter, I argued that when *Portrait of Edmond Belamy* speculates on the relegation of creative agency to AI, it proceeds strategically. The work aligns AI art with the traditional value propositions of the art market, as well as with the humanist figuration of "author" on which it relies. Here, AI is not mobilized in an effort to form new types of agential assemblages that might critique and recalibrate existing property models. Rather, *Portrait of Edmond Belamy* utilizes GAN technology in a spirit of perpetuating and reinforcing the anthropocentric logic of cultural ownership in AI contexts. The controversy surrounding the work is, in this sense, also a reminder of how intellectual property (IP) discourse has always struggled, and often failed, to accommodate emerging technologies and their impact on the social and economic spheres within which and upon which they act (for influential critiques linked to this issue, see Coombe 1998; Vaidhyanathan 2001; Wirtén 2004; Lessig 2004; Halbert 2005; or McLeod 2007, among many others). This chapter turns to the Canadian artist Adam Basanta's AI-driven installation *All We'd Ever Need Is One Another* (2018), another AI art project that has provoked IP-related controversy. My aim is to explore how this particular project critiques established anthropocentric notions of creative agency that are expressed in contemporary IP models. In contrast to *Portrait of Edmond Belamy*, *All We'd Ever Need Is One Another* represents a step toward a more critically charged—tactical—utilization of AI, which embodies important characteristics of what I have earlier introduced as the posthumanist agential assemblage.

In my discussion of *Portrait of Edmond Belamy*, an implicit suggestion has been that there is a tendency, in current AI art, to resort to anthropocentric perspectives and analogies in attempts to frame non-human expressive agency. This can ultimately perpetuate humanist ideals of authorship and cultural ownership. By contrast, the playful invocation of the prospect of non-human creativity in *All We'd Ever Need Is One Another* provokes fundamental speculative challenges of such ideals. The installation forces a reconsideration of how AI-based expressive agency might interfere with established assumptions concerning authorship, as well as the ownership models IP law legitimates. As discussed below, this has also had the unintended consequence of a copyright infringement complaint against Basanta. Functioning as an independently operating "art factory" (Basanta 2018), the installation links approaches familiar from appropriation art with the notion of the autonomous, creative AI assemblage. In doing so, *All We'd Ever Need Is One Another* formulates an implicit critique of current IP conventions and their inability (now as always) to accommodate many of the new expressive modes that emerging digital technologies afford digital artists.

(In)validating Artfulness

All We'd Ever Need Is One Another was first exhibited in 2018 at Ellephant Gallery in Montreal (fig. 4). It has since gone through several iterations, and continues to be shown online as well

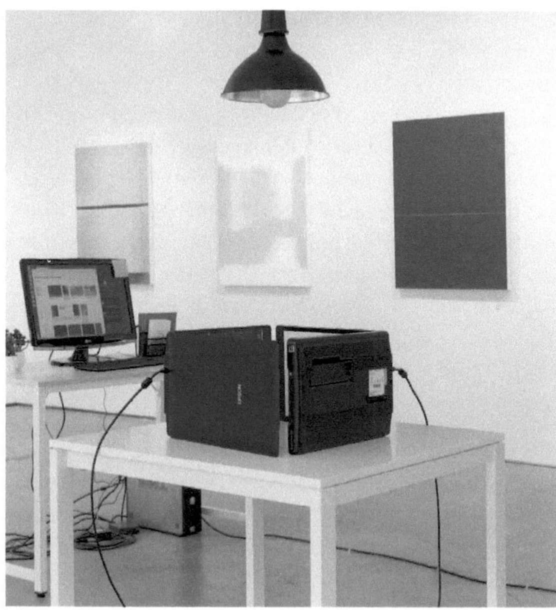

[Figure 4] Adam Basanta, installation view of *All We'd Ever Need Is One Another* (2018), Galerie ELLEPHANT, Montréal. Image used by permission of the artist; photo credit: Simon Belleau.

as in physical exhibition spaces (e.g., Arsenal Contemporary Toronto 2019). In its original form, the installation featured two flatbed scanners, a number of networked desktop computers, a large printer, as well as a project website and several social media accounts associated with the work. This setup constitutes a system capable of independently generating images in an automated multi-step process, and of instantiating these images as artworks both in material form (as printouts) and digitally (by distributing them online). During the exhibition at Ellephant Gallery, a limited run of images produced by the system were made available for sale as unique canvas prints; additionally, automatically generated printouts were available for sale as unique poster editions (in subsequent presentations, these prints accumulated on the gallery floor and were freely available for gallery visitors to take away). Overall, *All We'd Ever Need Is One Another* reveals itself quite clearly as an artwork that involves a human artist. But with regard to the generative aspects of the installation, especially those that reach beyond the work's material instantiation in an exhibition space, the project also casts doubt on the creative agency that this human artist is able to exercise during the creative process. In other words, the notion of authorial control does not easily attach to the functioning and outputs of *All We'd Ever Need Is One Another.* I would argue, in fact, that the work is conceptualized with the specific aim of eliminating, as completely as possible, all potential for human intervention in the generative process.

In this sense, a key characteristic of the project is precisely the kind of speculative decentering of expressive agency that I have described as an important aspect of the posthumanist agential assemblage. In the installation's generative processes, the notion of an independent, singular, supreme human creative agency from which the artwork originates is thus negated, or, at the very least, strongly put in doubt. This occurs in several steps. In the first step, the system generates images without relying on human input. It does so by using two (or more) flatbed scanners which are placed on their sides, so that their scanning surfaces face each other. Once turned on, the scanners are controlled by custom software that continuously puts the devices through successive scanning cycles. The software also randomizes the device settings between cycles, in such a way that their outputs vary dramatically without any need for additional manipulation or external (human) input. The setup of the scanner array thus eliminates the artist's ability to interfere with or control the scanning process itself; in the gallery setup, the arrangement of the scanners presents itself as a physical and visual barrier against interference, highlighting that human participation is effectively shut out. Suggestive of a kind of generative machine introspection, the devices only ever scan each other, or more precisely, they record distorted, unfocused light patterns that hit their glass surfaces, perhaps in the form of reflections bouncing off of the devices they are facing. The outputs thus generated do not rely on any source images, and Basanta estimates that the system can create between 1,000 and 1,500 images over a 24-hour period (roughly one every minute-and-a-half).

In the next step, these images are subjected to an automated validation process that is designed to identify presumptively artful images among the generated outputs. With regard to this process, Basanta has explained that if a scan is "similar enough to a work that the art market or international collections have deemed art-worthy, then that image, which is similar to it, is also art-worthy. It becomes art" (Hannay 2018). It strikes me as important that the threshold of "artworthiness" here is not simply an aesthetic measure: instead it is based on whether or not a matched work is circulating as a (more or less) valuable commodity. The system's validation process is thus directly linked to the art market dictate of commercial valorization. Basanta's art factory compares its outputs to existing artworks, and, in a tongue-in-cheek fashion, identifies some of its own randomly generated images as artful if—and only if—the installation recognizes them as satisfying a system-immanent similarity threshold. The system, in other words, is trained to consider its own outputs as artworks only if they register as "copies" of existing artworks. As I will go on to argue, this designation is not as straightforward as it may seem, and this complication is central to the critique of traditional ownership models that *All We'd Ever Need Is One Another* formulates.

The system-immanent validation process is carried out using a content recognition protocol that draws on a large image database of existing artworks. This database is assembled by a custom scraper tool that scans freely accessible online image repositories of existing artworks, and which collects relevant images as well as metadata such as the original artist's name, the title of the work, and the year it was created. Based on the dataset contents, this artificially intelligent system then searches for "matches" between the auto-generated scans and the collected images. While Basanta has noted that the system searches for matches that exceed 83% similarity, exhibitions of *All We'd Ever Need Is One Another* have not included detailed information regarding the precise parameters that would determine such a match. Anthropocentric and ocularcentric pragmatism might suggest that a match will occur when a generative output "looks like" an existing artwork. But importantly, in Basanta's system this is rarely the case. Thus, an additional conceptual twist is introduced, since *All We'd Ever Need Is One Another* does not appear to root its determinations of artfulness in standard definitions of "copy" and "original." Instead, an algorithmic process that focuses on parameters including aspect ratio, composition, form/shape detection, and color distribution across the canvas determines when a successful match has occurred. Importantly, this process relies on perceptual hashing algorithms that are used in medical imaging research and, notably, in automated copyright infringement detection. Overall, this highlights an intriguing implication, namely that the validation process based on which Basanta's system determines artfulness is not human-legible.

Details regarding the functionality of the search-and-match algorithm remain confined within the system itself. Like the blackbox of a proprietary algorithm, the decisions of *All We'd Ever Need Is One Another* are difficult to fathom for human observers. This could be taken as a nod to the inexplicability of the inner workings of many AI systems, in which, as I have noted earlier, blackboxing can occur as a strategy of corporate secrecy, as an IP-protection mechanism, or as a result of the sheer complexity of the computational processes that are being carried out by the system. In the given context of *All We'd Ever Need Is One Another*, I interpret the validation process as a playful invocation of the humanist notion of creative genius, in which the presumptive unknowability of a great artist's mind also constitutes a kind of blackboxing. Additionally, in Basanta's project the unknowable process of how an expression is validated as artful also involves the deletion of all generated images that don't match existing artworks. This inverts the conventional anthropocentric logic of creative expression: the system permits only matching items ("copies"?) to become instantiated as artworks, while non-matching items ("originals"?) are erased before ever taking human-legible form on screen or in print.

The successful matches (Basanta has noted that the system can produce between twenty and fifty per day) are then submitted to the final step in the auto-generative process, in which the outputs are furnished with titles that reference the matched artworks. This echoes established conventions familiar from appropriation art, whereby title, creator's name, and other details may be explicitly included in the appropriation itself. (For a well-known example, recall Sherrie Levine's series *After Walker Evans* from 1981, which consists of photographic reproductions of Depression-era photographs by Walker Evans). In Basanta's project, the full title of a finished piece includes the degree of similarity to its match, the name of the matched work's creator, the title of that work, and the year it was made. One example of an "artful" output of *All We'd Ever Need Is One Another* is thus titled *85.81%_match: Amel Chamandy 'Your World Without Paper', 2009*, and references a photographic artwork titled *Your World Without Paper* (2009), by the Canadian artist Amel Chamandy (the two images can be compared in fig. 5 and 6). To the human eye, the two images bear little resemblance, aside from a reliance on a shared color range that favors deep purple and bright pink hues. The suggestion encoded in the work's title—that the generative output is 85.81% identical to Chamandy's artwork—is certainly not immediately obvious to the human observer. It was enough, however, to provoke a complaint of copyright and trademark infringement, filed by Chamandy against Basanta in the Quebec Superior court in August of 2018 (the case is still pending at the time of writing).

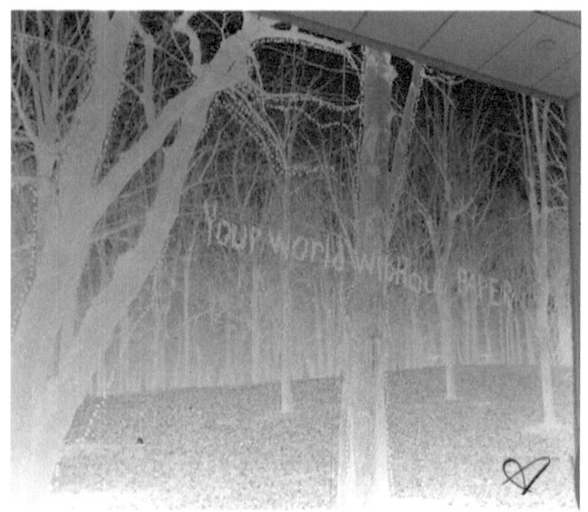

[Figure 5] Amel Chamandy, *Your World Without Paper* (2009). Copyright Amel Chamandy; image used by permission.

[Figure 6] Adam Basanta, *85.81%_match: Amel Chamandy 'Your World Without Paper', 2009* (2018). Image used by permission of the artist.

In the complaint, Chamandy alleges that Basanta's work violates her copyright in the photographic work *Your World Without Paper*, as well as a trademark registered in her name. Chamandy's copyright infringement allegation asserts, among other things, that "the process used by the Defendant to compare his computer generated images to Amel Chamandy's work necessarily required an unauthorized copy of such a work to be made" (Statement of Claim, para. 30, cited in Scassa 2018). In an email to Basanta, disclosed as part of the legal proceedings, the legal counsel representing Chamandy and NuEdge (a gallery she owns in Montreal), also wrote that the alleged infringement "illegally divert[s] internet traffic away from NuEdge's website and allows [Basanta] to unduly benefit from the goodwill and reputation associated with the name and trademark AMEL CHAMANDY" (Hannay 2018). In the original complaint, Chamandy claimed statutory damages of CAN$40,000 for the commercial misappropriation of her copyrighted work and her trademark; this has since then been updated to CAN$122,000, on the basis that many more of Chamandy's artworks were allegedly web-scraped and copied.

The explicit accusation here is two-fold: first, that the process by which the work in question was created involves the copying of Chamandy's work, and that the copying process was unauthorized and unfair; and second, that the project's invocation of Chamandy's name benefits Basanta and poses financial harm to her. In the context of my broader discussion, I note that the legal complaint seeks to frame this issue in a conventional IP context. This aligns with current legislation and the interests of the litigant, but it ignores the conceptual thrust of the allegedly infringing work, specifically its speculative exploration of a posthumanist, non-human form of creative expression that is incompatible with anthropocentric property enclosures. Evidently, any complaint operating within the established paradigms of human authorship must fail to address the question of what sort of creative agency and authorial control Adam Basanta can actually be argued to have had in the creation of the work in question.

A closer look at this legal dispute emphasizes the implicit critique levelled in *All We'd Ever Need Is One Another* against the aesthetic, ethical, and socio-economic assumptions underpinning prevailing IP models. Chamandy's complaint alleges that Basanta's use is commercial in nature. However, *85.81%_match: Amel Chamandy 'Your World Without Paper', 2009* is not for sale, and Basanta does not appear to derive advertisement income from his project website or the associated social media accounts (Scassa 2018). Chamandy's claim regarding the commercial nature of the appropriation is difficult to prove, but it also represents an inevitable necessity for the claimant's case: to acknowledge that Basanta's use is non-commercial in nature would likely disqualify the trademark infringement complaint, and support the conclusion that the copying undertaken as part of the generative process is covered by the Canadian Copyright Act's fair dealing exception (which outlines permissible, non-infringing uses of copyright-protected materials, including their copying and reusing).[1] In any case, Chamandy now faces the burden of having to show that Basanta drew direct commercial benefit from the alleged infringement—perhaps by having increased his reputation as an artist, or by improving his ability to attract funding for his practice; as the Canadian legal scholar Teresa Scassa (2018) has pointed out, such claims are exceedingly difficult to prove.[2]

1 'Fair dealing' and 'fair use' exemptions to copyright restrictions are discussed in more detail in the following chapter. For the moment, it suffices to note that while non-commercial uses are generally more likely to be considered fair (i.e., non-infringing), the commercial nature of a use is not necessarily a determinative factor in fair dealing deliberations.

2 The trademark allegation is very unlikely to have any merit, and I will not discuss it any further here. As another commentator has noted, "Chamandy will have the impossible task of proving that Basanta's use of her trademarked

Regarding the specifics of copyright infringement, a key question is whether Basanta himself has illegitimately undertaken the copying of *Your World Without Paper*. At first sight, there are several indications that this might be the case. In the art historical traditions of 20th century appropriation art, the referencing of a "source" work in the title of a new artwork tends to express an explicit and provocative admission that a copy was indeed made. In this sense, the title of the work in question could be understood as an indication that, firstly, the piece represents a copy that is 85.81% identical to Amel Chamandy's *Your World Without Paper* and, secondly, that it is indeed derivative in nature, since Chamandy's referenced original was, without doubt, created nine years prior to the alleged misappropriation. From this angle, Chamandy's legal perspective echoes the controversies that appropriation art has often provoked (many of them are collected, for example, in McClean and Schubert 2002, and in Evans 2009). The added speculative twist here is that the involvement of a non-human, artificially creative system might make it much harder to pin down who or what is responsible for the act of appropriation itself.

What the complaint does not acknowledge is the fundamentally dialogical and relational nature of Basanta's project, and of creative expression in general (including Chamandy's own practice). In this sense, *All We'd Ever Need Is One Another* can be well described using terminology used by Craig and Kerr: the artificially intelligent generative system at work here is marked by "relational autonomy" and enacts, at least speculatively, a form of "dialogic authorship" (2021, 83) that works across the different components of the system and the intertextual information on which it draws (see also Nedelsky 2011, on which the authors draw). In other words, insofar as *All We'd Ever Need Is One Another* is assumed to be capable of generating creative expressions, it

name to bolster his own reputation constitutes advertisement in association with a service" (Burrell 2019).

must be acknowledged that the system (both in its functionality and in its outputs) explicitly proposes that artworks exist in continuums in which they are linked to other, already-existing creative expressions as well as the agencies that produced them. This perspective is fundamentally at odds with Chamandy's legal complaint, which must construe *85.81%_match: Amel Chamandy 'Your World Without Paper', 2009* as an artwork created by a unified, human author figure on the basis of an intentional copying of her work.

In my reading, *All We'd Ever Need Is One Another* destabilizes conventional assumptions regarding what it means to create artworks in AI contexts, and, by extension, what it means to copy and to own creative expressions in such contexts. As noted, Chamandy's allegation hinges on the idea that Basanta has created an unauthorized copy. However, the offending image results from generative processes that make it not only unnecessary, but in fact impossible for Basanta himself to participate or intervene in its creation in a conventional sense. Functioning as an independent art factory, the project quite plainly cuts the traditional author figure out of the equation. Conceptually and practically (if not legally), the setup of the installation disqualifies Basanta as the default creator of any of its image outputs, including the disputed image. *All We'd Ever Need Is One Another* constitutes a posthumanist agential assemblage in which the human artist is participant rather than creator. Basanta's role is decentered, and his capacity to function as author is significantly limited. Within the speculative framework of how the installation operates, this puts into doubt the human artist's responsibility for the alleged infringing action.

The human participant's creative agency is here negated by design, since the generative processes of *All We'd Ever Need Is One Another* are shielded from his interference such that he cannot direct, anticipate, or control the outputs (unless, perhaps, if he were to turn the entire system off). Both from a legal and from a philosophical perspective, this raises a difficult question that is of broader interdisciplinary interest in current AI discourse: to which extent can Basanta be held liable for an alleged infringing action even when it is agreed that he did not "author" the offending image, but merely "authorized" an autonomous machinic action that happened to result in its production? With a focus on the aesthetics and conceptual thrust of the installation, it seems less than certain that Basanta can be called the author of *85.81%_match: Amel Chamandy 'Your World Without Paper', 2009*. I would argue, on the contrary, that an important design feature of Basanta's installation is precisely to permit the human agent involved in its operation "deniability" with regard to their presumptive authorial control over the outputs.

At least two speculative defences against Chamandy's allegation of copyright infringement are conceivable. A first line of defence could be for Basanta to claim, simply, "I have no agency with regard to the creation of the image; I am not its author." As noted in a previous chapter, most copyright legislation currently presumes human agency as a prerequisite for any creative expression to be legally recognized as authored. The speculative implication here is that if that the possibility of non-human creative agency is taken seriously, it will become difficult to assert the sole accountability and culpability of human agents who play peripheral roles in shared creative processes. If, in response to such an argument, it is objected that Basanta has, after all, designed and built *All We'd Ever Need Is One Another* for the specific purpose of creating near-identical matches of already-existing artworks, and that he uses the AI-based validation process merely as an instrument for this process, a further retort comes to mind: since the matches are validated on a machine-readable spectrum of similarity that isn't legible to the human perceptual apparatus, they cannot be said to constitute copies in a sense that fits with anthropocentric, ocularcentric ontologies of "similarity" that human agents can meaningfully interpret as such. In this sense, the creation of *85.81%_match: Amel Chamandy*

 'Your World Without Paper', 2009 involved no copying of a kind that IP law or theories of art could recognize.

These objections can form the basis for a second line of critical defence, this one focusing more directly on how the artistic use of AI technology problematizes aesthetic and legal perspectives on the nature of originality, copying and, by extension, creativity. Technically speaking, the consumer-grade scanners used for *All We'd Ever Need Is One Another* are high-resolution copy machines designed to reproduce images to a very high degree of accuracy. But in the specific constellation of Basanta's project, this standard purpose of the scanner—quite simply to render copies of originals at the behest of the human agents who operate them—is undermined. In this particular context, the images created by these high-precision copying devices must themselves be regarded as originals, since no input is required and no source is ever reproduced. In relation to Chamandy's claim, this means that the similarity registered in the validation process does not follow the sequential logic normally associated with a copying activity, according to which a pre-existing original is copied to create a derivative. Instead, the generative process employed here renders outputs that are always "original," just as the outputs of generative GAN-style systems (as discussed in the previous chapter) cannot be meaningfully perceived as "copies" of their training dataset contents.

As noted, *All We'd Ever Need Is One Another* begins by outputting random images, some of which are then validated as artworks through the use of an automated comparative process that involves pre-existing artworks. But importantly, the link between the installation's outputs and the pre-existing artworks is drawn in a retrospective manner, enacting an inversion of the conventional causality of "original" and "copy." There is no doubt that the creation of the pre-existing artwork with which a scan might be matched predates the creation of the scan itself (in other words, Chamandy clearly created her artwork nine years before Basanta built and activated a system that then produced and validated the matching output). But this temporal ordering alone does not in itself mean that the output of Basanta's system is indeed a derivative or transformative work. This is because the image was generated with no *a priori* knowledge of Chamandy's pre-existing artwork: the similarity between the two emerges only after the fact. In copyright law, such an observation can fuel a so-called "independent creation" defence. This refers to a scenario in which reproduction of a copyright-protected creative expression occurs without awareness of the existence of the original, with the consequence that the new expression may not legally constitute a copy at all.[3] A legal opinion by the American judge and philosopher of law Learned Hand (1872–1961) summarizes this conundrum well: "if by some magic a man who had never known it were to compose anew Keat's *Ode to a Grecian Urn*, he would be an 'author,' and, if he copyrighted it, others may not copy that poem, though they might of course copy Keat's" (*Sheldon v. Metro-Goldwyn Pictures Corp.*, 1936; the passage has been invoked by many legal scholars—see, for example, Saint-Amour 2003 and Patry 2005). Following this logic, outputs created by the complex pseudo-copy machine that *All We'd Ever Need Is One Another* constitutes are therefore no copies at all, regardless of the degree of their claimed similarity to other artworks.

Updating Learned Hand's dictum to the digital context within which *All We'd Ever Need Is One Another* operates, I would argue the following: in this particular situation, the disputed image was created by a hardware-software-human agential assemblage that contains a sandboxed generative system. This system operates in isolation, without knowledge of the pre-existing works to which its outputs might later be matched. Technically, this system can ever only churn out originals, since creative copying requires some foreknowledge, i.e., a kind of intertextual awareness, or at least embeddedness in a relational system

3 On emerging questions concerning the applicability of independent creation defences in AI contexts, see Asay 2020.

of signification (cf. Sanders 2006, discussed in Zeilinger 2009). The generative components of *All We'd Ever Need Is One Another* are specifically denied such access. In the end, it is only the referential titling convention employed in Basanta's system that makes its outputs human-legible as "copies." This conceptual stance appeals provocatively to the anthropocentric sensibilities of human audiences, habituated as they are to relatively clear-cut differentiation between original and copy. In this case, however, the particular relationship between the system's outputs and the existing artworks to which they are matched undermines this differentiation, since no clear view is provided on where and how creative agency is situated in the installation.

Copying and Human-Non-Readability

As it stands, the legal complaint against Basanta might succeed on the granular level of scrutinous doctrinal analysis, if it focuses on legal definitions of copying activities in technological systems. The infringement allegation hinges on the assertion that even though Basanta may not have published or commercially distributed copies of Chamandy's artwork, a copy of this work must surely have been made as part of the database used in the automated validation process of scans. This argument targets a blind spot in existing legislation regarding the legality of copying processes as part of data-mining and data-analysis activities (Scassa 2018; Burrell 2019; Guihot and Rimmer 2019; Sag 2019). These processes tend to occur on a computational level and are not directly facilitated, accessed, or even perceived by human agents. Consequently, their legal status is, for now, not entirely clear. Chamandy's complaint implies that such processes—specifically the automated, quasi-non-human copying undertaken by the scraper tool as part of the validation process—violate her copyright. But if this perspective can be upheld, many of the copying processes on which machine learning fundamentally relies would also become subject to legal contestation.

It is self-evident that the matching between the disputed output of *All We'd Ever Need Is One Another* and Chamandy's artwork could only occur if the generative system had access to a copy of her image. It is uncertain, however, whether this use (unauthorized though it may be) is indeed illicit. Writing in the U.S. context, the law and technology scholar Matthew Sag (2019) argues that "non-expressive uses" of expressive works, of the kind that occur in data-mining for machine learning purposes, should be considered as fair uses to avoid fundamental conflicts between copyright law and "copy-reliant technologies" (cf. Sag 2009). If data-mining for machine learning purposes were to be regarded as an infringing copying activity, this would cast considerable doubt on the legality not only of art projects such as Basanta's, but also, for example, on key practices in the digital humanities, from Franco Moretti's "distant reading" through Paul Martin Eve's computational close reading techniques to Lev Manovich's "cultural analytics" (see Moretti 2000, also Ascari 2014; Eve 2019; Manovich 2020).

This would also problematize the legal status of most GAN-based art that relies on Internet-scraped training data. The only exceptions would then be formed by the work of AI artists who use custom-compiled, "original" training data, such as Helena Sarin and Anna Ridler, who have argued that this approach enables them to retain artistic control over the resulting generative outputs (see Zeilinger 2021). For now, it remains unclear whether unauthorized compilation and use of copyright-protected material for AI training purposes indeed amounts to copyright infringement. Conventionally, such infringement is characterized not only by the production of unauthorized copies, but also by their publication and distribution. But copies created for data mining and machine learning purposes are rarely circulated in this way. In the case of *All We'd Ever Need Is One Another*, for example, scraped data is not technically published or distributed, since the source materials are never compiled for human use. Here, the copyright-protected data is "perceived"—i.e., read, viewed, or otherwise interpreted—only by a computational system, and it is doubtful whether such a use can be easily characterized as infringing.

Scassa has noted that challenging the legitimacy of this kind of copying activity "opens a window into the potential impact of statutory damages in text and data mining activities" (2018). If the compilation of datasets that are ever only machine-readable were to become subject to narrowly interpreted copyright restrictions (on the basis of restrictions that already apply to human readers), there can be no doubt that the same chilling effects that expansive IP regimes already have on human expressive agency will also negatively impact AI. An avalanche of legal actions brought against those who design the automated compilation, circulation, or use of such datasets—and more importantly, against those who own or control them—would likely follow.[4] Within the conceptual framework of AI art I am outlining in this book, I would argue that allegations of illegitimate copying such as Chamandy's have little merit. To highlight the complicated relationship between AI art and traditional notions of authorship

4 Tech corporations and research institutions have already begun to respond to such concerns. This is evident in recent deletions of large datasets that had been widely used for research and training purposes in machine vision. When it was reported, in early 2019, that the commercially used dataset MS-Celeb-1M, owned by Microsoft Corporation, contained roughly 10 million images of about 100,000 individuals harvested from online sources, it took only a few days before online access to the dataset was removed; Duke University and Stanford University followed suit and took down two other large datasets of similar type, called Duke MTMC and Brainwash, respectively (see Murgia 2019a, 2019b). Officially undertaken because of privacy concerns, the deletions also indicate growing uncertainty regarding the IP status of database contents. As the *Financial Times* reported, MS-Celeb-1M only harvested images covered by Creative Commons (CC) licenses; it is not clear, however, what specific CC licenses (some of which expressly prohibit commercial use) were attached to the images. A research paper published by Microsoft software engineers involved in building the dataset does not clarify this point, and refers only to the use of "freebase" data, i.e., content from a Google-owned (now-defunct) entity that has since been replaced by Google's Knowledge Base (see Guo at al. 2016).

and ownership is precisely the point of tactical uses of AI as I am discussing them. Here, new types of posthumanist techniques of reproduction and creative expression emerge, and it is not surprising that the logic of IP, with its anthropocentric prioritization of conventional property enclosures, cannot easily accommodate them.

It is unclear how the law will ultimately deal with the kind of massive-scale, gray-area data appropriation that corporations and research institutions have undertaken for years. There will likely be a move toward regulating big data mining and analysis, for example by creating IP licensing schemes that govern the use of dataset contents. But this will almost certainly occur against the background of economic considerations, rather than with a focus on cultural implications. The problematic effects of this can already be observed in some isolated instances. For example, the publisher Elsevier—notorious in academic circles for its relentless pursuit of outlandishly high profit margins—appears to have realized that regulation of data-mining allows for the creation of a new revenue stream for corporate content owners, and has designed new subscription solutions to re-monetize its vast portfolio of digitized texts for use in AI training applications (Elsevier n.d.).

In contrast to these developments, the UK Supreme Court has fairly recently re-asserted the argument that intra-computational activities of viewing, reading, and other forms of data-analysis are not likely to constitute copyright infringement (UKSC 18, 2013). In line with this perspective, UK copyright law already provides an important exception to copyright restrictions that allows the copying of works "for text and data analysis," as long as the analysis is "for the purpose of non-commercial research" and the copy is, where reasonably possible, "accompanied by sufficient acknowledgment" (UK Copyright and Rights in Performances Regulations 2014, section 29A). In a roundabout way, this dovetails with the view that "machine reading" is non-infringing, and also neatly inverts the meaning of Grimmelmann's suggestion, as cited earlier, that copyright law is "for humans only" (2016, 674).

On this basis, I would argue that the kind of computational viewing and reading of web-scraped content that characterizes the functionality of *All We'd Ever Need Is One Another* must be considered to be permissible. The use is non-commercial, the vast majority of the used material never leaves the blackbox of the system itself, and those images that the system validates as artful are immediately furnished with a clear acknowledgment of the referenced work. As a posthumanist agential assemblage capable of generating outputs that can be interpreted as creative (or which are, in any case, framed as such), *All We'd Ever Need Is One Another* enacts a kind of creativity that is unknowable in anthropocentric paradigms of originality, human creative labor, or original genius. Consequently, it is perhaps also unrecognizable within the legal systems that these paradigms have spawned. Ultimately, it is only thanks to the system's own validation process and titling convention, which exteriorizes the generative outputs as human-legible (i.e., labelled) artefacts, that any infringement allegation becomes possible at all. But by invoking appropriation art practices, the same process also places the outputs within an ontology of art that operates beyond the traditional logic of copy and original.

In the realm of creative expression, the speculative *post hoc* "anti-copying" of *All We'd Ever Need Is One Another* is reminiscent of other thought experiments that complicate the logic of original creation and appropriation. The "infinite monkey theorem," for example, postulates that a group of monkeys sat at typewriters will, if given enough time, end up (re)writing William Shakespeare's entire body of work in the form of randomly assembled texts that cannot technically be regarded as copies (cf. Hattenbach and Glucoft 2015). Jorge Luis Borges' short story *Pierre Menard, Author of the Quixote*, raises the same question in a different constellation: the story is about the chance rewriting of Cervantes' *Don Quixote*, authored by a writer named

Pierre Menard who worked without any prior knowledge of the already-existing novel (Borges 1941). As Borges' protagonist argues, Menard's text is no copy at all, but a sensational artistic achievement that must be accepted as an entirely new work, even though it matches the prior expression down to the last comma. Like Basanta's project, Borges' short story forces a reconsideration of the deceptively simple question of how an original might be defined, what constitutes a copy, and what significance these definitions bear on our understanding of creativity, as well as of the identity, responsibilities, and ownership rights of an author figure.

But there is also a key difference here, and this, again, points beyond human-legible ontologies of expressive agency. In Borges' story, readers are invited to suspend their disbelief, and to try to accept two plainly identical works, created by two separate human agents, as equally original. By contrast, Adam Basanta's art factory produces matches that are not easily identifiable as such to the human eye. Here, the matches exist first of all in and for the "eye" of the machine, and are interpreted not for the sake of a human observer, but for that of a closed-circuit computational system. Only in the very last step of the validation process is the output reified as artful in a human-legible sense. It strikes me as important that this does not occur through the specialized agency of someone like an art critic (as in Manovich's AI art Turing test, which, as I have argued in a previous chapter, amplifies anthropocentric bias instead of dissolving it), or a literary scholar (as in Borges' short story). Instead, in the case of *All We'd Ever Need Is One Another* it is the computational system itself that reifies its outputs for human audiences. I would describe this as a tactical inversion of the anthropocentric framing discussed by Craig and Kerr. Instead of human agents framing AI systems such that they can fit with anthropocentric notions of intelligence or creativity, here the generative system frames its own outputs in such a way that they become recognizable as art (and perhaps delegitimized as copies) for an all-too human audience.

[6]

From Non-Human Agency to Human Non-Agency: Creative Expression in the Age of Algorithmic Copyright Enforcement

Is human agency the "ghost in the machine" of AI art, something that can be conjured rhetorically, or is it hidden inside a computational blackbox, and not easily erased? My discussion throughout the previous chapters has implied that spectacularizing stories of a becoming-creative of non-human computational entities are naively overwrought. Undeniably, human expressive agency persists in digital art that is produced with and by AI—as is evident, for example, in Anna Ridler's emphasis on artist-compiled datasets, in the manifold interventions enacted by Obvious Collective in its use of a GAN system, and even in Adam Basanta's design of an art factory that speculatively cuts the human artist out of the creativity equation. In any case, as Joanna Zylinska (2020) also notes, to ask whether computers can be creative is a misguided question. What I have been asking instead is how expressive agency is being redistributed in artificially intelligent agential assemblages, and how, consequently, the concepts of agency and creative expression have become subject to critical recalibrations. I have asked, in other words, how AI acts upon human creative agency, and what the critical stakes of this impact are. My proposition has been that the agential assemblages through which AI art emerges can operate tactically, along posthumanist vectors that decenter romantic fictions of human authorship and creative genius, and which thus also disturb the integrity of ownership models building on these fictions. But conversely, AI can also be deployed strategically, and perpetuate the humanist ideal of singular, unified human agency that translates so easily into narrow conceptions of authorship and restrictive norms of cultural ownership. As a specific example of this kind of strategic AI deployment, YouTube's AI-based digital rights management (DRM) tool Content ID is the subject of this chapter.

Content ID is a proprietary tool designed to enforce YouTube's corporate perspective on copyright policy. Access to its functionality is sold as a subscription service to large scale content owners. Since Content ID and the YouTube platform itself operate in the realm of mass media, the following analysis broadens the scope of my discussion beyond the speculative interventions that digital art can stage when it uses AI tactically. But my discussion will also frequently link back to Adam Basanta's art factory, discussed in the previous chapter, in order to draw out significant contrasts between the reconceptualization of appropriation techniques present in *All We'd Ever Need Is One Another*, and the property-oriented operational logic of a copyright enforcement tool such as Content ID. Both, I will argue, represent new types of agential assemblages in which agency is redistributed across human and non-human entities. However, the two systems form conceptual inversions of one another, with the former engaging AI tactically to open up new horizons of expressive agency, and the latter proceeding strategically to streamline and amplify restrictive intellectual property (IP) enclosures.

In elaborating these contrasts, my discussion of corporate IP perspectives and mainstream entertainment media feeds back into my broader points concerning the impact of AI on issues of agency and ownership, and, by extension, concerning the critical potential of AI in these contexts. Like the art projects discussed in the previous chapters, Content ID sits at the intersection between questions of expressive agency, AI, and IP. But there is a crucial difference: whereas a work such as *All We'd Ever Need Is One Another* uses AI to problematize the notion that unified, singular agency is embodied in the author-*qua*-owner, the purpose of Content ID is instead to amplify the idea of singular, unified authorship, which it reifies in its algorithmic enforcement of over-simplified IP enclosures. Functioning as a blackboxed computational system furnished with the power to monitor, analyze, and impede human expressive agency, Content ID effectively forecloses even the speculative possibility of the posthumanist agential assemblage in the broader digital cultural landscape.

In my discussion of Adam Basanta's work in the previous chapter, the construction of such an assemblage, and the proposition that it can shield the system's presumptively creative processes from human intervention, has framed a kind of deniability of human creative agency. But this should not distract from the fact that even in such a construct, a human participant's relinquishing of their authorial control remains an enactment of expressive agency. Artists' efforts to erase their own authorial control are familiar from conceptual art, surrealism, certain tendencies within computer art, and many artforms that rely on chance operations. When creative expression interfaces with algorithmic DRM tools, however, the divestment of agency is no longer necessarily a conceptual stance: now, it may be imposed on human agents, rather than being adopted by them. When powerful AI systems become governance tools (whether in surveillance, commercial contexts, or law enforcement), they begin to act upon human agency in a capacity that can take on more or less automated and autonomous forms. AI-driven DRM systems are a case in point. They instrumentalize AI for the purpose of monitoring and controlling expressive activity, and are ultimately capable of curtailing or even outright denying agency, even before something such as a creative expression can ever be instantiated in human-readable form. Many everyday internet users will likely have experienced this first hand, when their attempts to upload audio or video content containing "non-original" elements to platforms such as YouTube, Facebook, or Twitter were automatically denied by an algorithmic DRM system.

In such contexts, what I have discussed in chapter 3 as the Hegelian exteriorization of the self cannot occur in the first place, because the DRM system interprets an upload as the attempted authoring of a digital artefact that may trespass on the intellectual property of another author. In the logic of Hegel's personality theory, this also means the denial of an expression that would be co-constitutive of an individual's personhood and agency. In IP contexts, this can be rephrased as follows: if copyright norms are algorithmically encoded such that they can be monitored by and enforced through AI systems, a problematic shift occurs—away from the potential emergence of new forms of non-human expressive agency embodied in AI, and toward new forms of human non-agency enacted through AI.

The rights afforded by copyright law are intended to foster creativity, to protect artists' interests, and to safeguard the integrity of authored works. In this sense, copyright itself can be understood as a mechanism for administering, regulating, and protecting expressive agency, something that the law aims to do by granting certain exclusive rights to authors. But in order to achieve this equitably and fairly, copyright cannot be absolute or perpetual, and must be limited both in scope and duration. These limits are crucial for the law to be able to effect a finely calibrated balance between the IP rights of content owners, and the access rights and needs of those whose expressive capabilities rely on the use of potentially copyright-protected materials (including artists, researchers, or journalists). It is understood, in other words, that if the restrictions encoded in copyright law are too extensive or too rigid, they may be able to protect the economic interests of content owners more efficiently (and more profitably), but they will then have a chilling effect on the benefits any community can derive from the creativity and expressive agency of its members.

To avoid this, copyright law seeks not only to protect artists from having their IP rights infringed, but also to ensure that IP rights do not unfairly impact the expressive agency of others. Ideally, this is achieved through exceptions to the restrictions imposed by the law. These exceptions are designed to permit "fair" access to and "fair" uses of copyright-protected materials, even where such uses are not authorized by rights holders; in fact, the exceptions make it unnecessary for users to obtain authorization from legally recognized authors and owners. In the United States, these exceptions are covered by the "fair use" doctrine; in the U.K. and other Commonwealth jurisdictions, similar exceptions are covered by the principle of "fair dealing." While there are important differences between the two legal constructs, both encode the idea that the IP enclosures imposed on creative practice must leave room for purposes that are central to the performance or enactment of expressive agency. In contemporary copyright law, such purposes tend to include criticism, educational use, and research, as well as new, often born-digital forms of creative expression that rely fundamentally on the copying and reusing of existing aesthetic artefacts (such as sampling, remixing practices, and other forms of user-generated content)."[1] Copyright law's fairness exceptions, in other words,

1 For a survey of fair use issues in the context of cultural production and creative expression, see Aufderheide and Jaszi 2018; for a collection of critical perspectives on fair dealing issues, see Coombe, Wershler and Zeilinger 2014. As noted, the concepts of fair use and fair dealing are not interchangeable, but share important similarities. In principle, all copyright law embodies the idealistic (and idealized) notion that creative expression is to be encouraged and fostered for common good. This encouragement, it is assumed, can be achieved by creating incentives for expressive activities. In utilitarian perspectives on copyright law, the incentive is economic in nature, and takes the form of limited-term exploitation rights, which allow the author/creator/owner of a copyright-protected artefact to reap the rewards of the intellectual labour that went into the creation of the artefact.

are meant to protect expressive agency from undue restrictions in the form of overreaching IP enclosures. But digital contexts pose difficult problems for how these ideals can continue to be meaningfully applied, both in theory and in practice. In the previous chapter, I identified the compilation and analysis of data for "machine reading" purposes as one area in which the applicability of fair use and fair dealing rules remains uncertain.

In my view, expressive activities that test the limits of what IP law considers fair constitute a crucially important enactment of expressive agency. This is evidenced, for example, in the many conceptual and legal disputes that have been (and continue to be) provoked by appropriation art in its many forms. Arguably, appropriation can yield its most powerful critiques of IP regimes not simply because it may interfere with legally recognized ownership rights, but also because it challenges the humanist foundations on which the conceptualization of these rights rests. The ability to defend allegedly infringing expressions and practices as fair is itself an important performance of expressive agency. When this is felt to be impeded by the law, copyright is sometimes critiqued as a contemporary form of economically motivated censorship that functions on the basis of wide-ranging restrictions of creative practices (see Sunder 1996; Vaver 2006; Coombe, Wershler and Zeilinger 2014; Tehranian 2015). Fair use and fair dealing are thus situated at the conflicted interface between expressive agency and its legal regulation. They delineate the conceptual and practical limits of the reach of IP law, and of the exclusive rights of copyright owners. As such, when expressive agency is in conflict with the enclosures of IP regimes, it contributes importantly both to the production of and the critical reflection on what the interdisciplinary humanities scholar Jane M. Gaines has called the propertization of "contested culture" (1991). As I have suggested throughout the previous chapters, in the context of AI these issues can take on the additional significance of exploring new figurations of the very concept of agency, along with the potential impact on existing ownership models.

Because each creative expression differs from the next in its form, intention, purpose, scope, etc., there can be no hard rules by which to easily determine whether an expression's use of copyright-protected materials is fair. To accommodate this complexity, the copyright exceptions encapsulated in the fair use and fair dealing definitions are formulated such that they can be "subject to varying methods of interpretation;" they are, in other words, "described in a vague and general manner in order to allow a flexible, case-by-case analysis" (Zygmunt 2016, 56). Crucially, this means that the law intends for any determination of whether an unauthorized use of copyright-protected materials can be considered fair to be difficult to undertake. Unsurprisingly, such determinations will depend on the context-specific assessment of many factors that vary from one example to another (Burk 2019, 287).

Determining fairness on a case-by-case basis is complicated and time-consuming, in part because most copyright statutes include formulations designed to make straightforward, rule-driven copyright adjudication virtually impossible. As such, fair use and fair dealing delineate complex and dynamic norms and standards that reflect shared social values concerning expressive agency and cultural ownership. This represents what I described in the introductory chapter as a crucially important interface between law, culture, and technology. As legal tools, fair use and fair dealing form counterpoints both to the restrictions that copyright law is capable of imposing on creative expression, and to the property enclosures that the law prescribes. In a cultural landscape dominated by rigid and vigorously enforced IP enclosures, creative expression that relies on fair use and fair dealing exceptions can therefore be understood as a powerful, but also inherently risky performance of creative agency.

 All of this is further complicated when AI is additionally taken into consideration. AI-driven DRM systems require that complex legal norms and standards regarding the fairness of expressive copying activities are encoded in much-simplified rules that can be enforced algorithmically. By necessity, any effort to do so must rely in part on problematic assumptions regarding the "effectively computable" nature of creativity. But a perspective that is critical of such assumptions suggests that it may be impossible for AI systems to deliberate fairly on the legality of creative expressions that draw on copyright-protected materials, and that an extremely problematic curtailing and recalibration of expressive agency may be the inevitable result.

Minimally Agential DRM and the Blackboxing of Copyright Adjudication

I have suggested that Adam Basanta's artificially intelligent art factory is designed to speculatively play up the non-human and post-humanist aspects of the expressive agency embodied in the system. The result is that at least conceptually, it becomes difficult to sustain conventional allegations of copyright infringement directed solely at a human participant identified as a singular, unified author figure (in this case, the artist). But what are the critical stakes of relegating agency to a non-human system in cultural contexts that reach beyond artistic experimentation? What if a blackboxed, minimally agential DRM tool is tasked with the quasi-adjudication of copyright, and in the process becomes a kind of "anti-art factory"? On the basis of invoking humanist ideals of creativity and originality and the restrictive cultural ownership models to which they lend themselves, such a system is likely to determine that whenever "copying" of any sort is detected, the rights of narrowly conceived author figures are being infringed upon. Importantly, in the outsourcing of such determinative processes to algorithmic systems, it becomes difficult to mount and sustain defences against infringement allegations.

This can be observed very clearly on online platforms such as YouTube, which serve as repositories for user-generated content (UGC). Content ID, the proprietary AI-driven DRM tool used by YouTube to determine the permissibility of creative expressions uploaded to the platform, encapsulates this issue perfectly. First deployed in 2007, Content ID is an automated filtering system designed as a corporate response to what was perceived as a rising tide of copyright-infringing uploads. The system automatically compares submitted content to a vast database containing "digital fingerprints" of existing, copyright-protected content.[2] If matches are found, the submitted content is flagged as a probable copyright infringement, after which the presumed rights holder can affirm or reverse this automated decision.[3] As a dynamic filtering system that effectively converts copyright adjudication into a privatized form of algorithmic content management, Content ID is an early example of a broader

2 The functionality of Content ID relies on a growing archive of metadata that uniquely identifies copyright-protected materials including films, TV content, and sound-based works. Rightsholders who wish to make use of the service must provide this information for reference, and the dataset used to train the Content ID system now contains over 50 million reference files, which allows the system to handle 98% of the YouTube platform's copyright management (e.g., Titlow 2016). Incidentally, copyright is not the only area in which YouTube employs such technologies. The platform has noted that a similar percentage of videos removed due to extremist content is also flagged by machine-learning algorithms (Wojcicki 2017).

3 Here is a more detailed outline of how a Content ID infringement claim unfolds: once the system has flagged content as infringing, the uploader can either "(a) accept the restrictions or (b) dispute the claim. If the claim is disputed, the rights holder has 30 days to either (a) release the claim or (b) uphold the claim. From here, the user can either (a) accept the restrictions or (b) issue an appeal. At this point, the rights holder can either (a) release the claim or (b) submit a DMCA notice" (Edwards 2018, 70).

 trend[4] toward AI-based copyright enforcement that can also be described as "AI-driven negative speech control" (Wu 2019, 2016).

Certain kinds of copyright infringement, such as the uploading of an entire music video, will be easy to recognize for even the most minimally agential DRM system. But a growing body of legal research challenges, as a matter of principle, the idea that AI-based tools are capable of identifying "fair" exceptions to copyright restrictions. Fair use and fair dealing, as I have noted, are designed to carve out exceptions in areas where the limits imposed by copyright law on expressive agency would otherwise be excessive. In this context, it is important to note that fair use and fair dealing can only be invoked in defence of an expression that has already been made (when it has been "published" and "perceived," to use the juridical terminology), and once its creator has been accused of infringement. This means that the fairness of an unauthorized use of copyright-protected materials can technically not be a certainty until an infringement complaint has been raised and rejected (the reverse is also true: the success of an infringement allegation may depend on the defeat of a fair use/fair dealing defence). This is sometimes interpreted as a conceptual weakness of copyright exceptions, based on the assumption that a more prescriptive, clearly defined set of permitted uses or "user rights" could offer reliable guidance regarding what constitutes infringement. Against this perspective, I would argue that the law's inclusive and open-ended formulations are precisely what empowers creativity and encourages its proactive enactment (these issues are discussed, for example, in Elkin-Koren 2017 and 2019). After all, what is the defence of an unauthorized use as fair, if not a critical performance of expressive agency? And what, in turn, is the relegation of

4 Facing issues concerning the need to monitor overwhelming amounts of UGC, many platforms have developed their own tools, so that by 2017, "platforms employing AI-driven, automated copyright enforcement schemes included Scribid, 4shared, Dropbox, YouTube, Facebook, SoundCloud, Twitch, TuneCore, Tumblr, Veoh, and Vimeo" (Sag 2017, 539).

copyright enforcement capabilities to an algorithmic system that is blind to such defences, if not a problematic enacting of human non-agency through AI means?

Recent analyses of Content ID in legal scholarship highlight a number of problematic issues pointing in this direction. To begin with, Content ID shares a key characteristic with many machine learning applications, namely the potential to improve the efficiency of its functionality over time. In the given context, this means that over time, the system will be able to identify presumptive infringement in ever more minute details of the content it analyzes (Heldt 2019, 61). The system may as a consequence become more difficult to circumvent, as its filtering processes are also taking on a self-reinforcing quality. Previous determinations of infringement are likely to shape future determinations, especially when the decisions are not disputed. Over time, Content ID can therefore get better at identifying what it perceives as infringement, but its mistakes will also be amplified. This is important because Content ID cannot, of course, detect infringement as such; it is capable only of mutely recognizing matches between value patterns in newly submitted content and the training dataset of reference files (Burk 2019, 297). Framed in the language of Crawford and Paglen (2019b) and many critics of algorithmic governance, this means that the determinations of Content ID are characterized by self-amplifying biases through which, in this case, decisions of a minimally agential computational system designed to monitor creative expressions will be experienced as law.

Another concern is that the inner workings of AI-driven DRM tools are generally blackboxed, either as a result of corporate strategy to protect valuable proprietary technology, or also because they are part of computational processes that are simply so complex that they are no longer legible for human agents (on this subject see Berry 2019, Deeks 2019, Pasquale 2015). Algorithmic adjudication of copyright offences is thus prone to "limits of explainability," in the sense that software "can often explain how it reached a decision, but not why" (Wu 2019, 2021). Here, algorithmic adjudication directly contradicts ideals of legal philosophy according to which the prescriptions of the law must remain human-comprehensible. Calls for AI explainability, in this sense, mirror the ideal of explainable jurisprudence. Systems such as Content ID, by contrast, represent what the sociology and technology scholar Zeynep Tufekci calls "stealthy gatekeepers," whose operations are "unaccompanied by transparency and visibility" (Tufekci 2015, cit. in Edwards 2018). Notably, when Content ID flags an upload as infringing, this process does not automatically initialize a formal copyright dispute. The legal procedure that normally accompanies a copyright complaint, and which is designed to safeguard the expressive agency of the accused, here becomes an algorithmically enacted, automated process that I would describe as no more than para-legal in nature. Conceptually, this extends the blackboxing of copyright adjudication from monitoring into the domain of enforcement, i.e., from the domain of the execution of software code to that of the enforcing of legal code. This also means that it can become entirely impossible for the uploader to enact the expressive agency that copyright law would afford them, in the form of their right to defend their use of the material as fair.

This curtailing of agency is veiled by an economically motivated procedural aspect of how Content ID functions. Ultimately, the goal of YouTube's corporate copyright enforcement strategy is not the deletion of offending material, but rather its monetization. In YouTube's business model, both the content owner and the platform operator derive income whenever users access uploaded material and watch the advertisements that frame the content. It is therefore in the interest of content owners and the platform owners that uploads remain online, even when it is alleged that they infringe copyright law. When, following the automatic flagging of uploaded content, a rightsholder decides that the material does indeed infringe their copyright, they are nevertheless incentivized to allow publication of the content, because they can then claim any advertisement-related income derived from page visits.

This might appear to be a good solution in theory: infringing material is allowed to remain accessible, the rightsholder receives a share of the advertisement revenue as compensation for the commercial harm that the infringement might otherwise cause them—everybody wins. But in reality, as the IP scholar Matthew Sag argues, this leads to a negative feedback loop that encourages rightsholders to permit publication of materials that are conveniently flagged as infringing by a biased algorithmic system, while users will be indirectly discouraged from appealing the AI system's decision since their content is, after all, allowed to remain online (2017, 541f). This may give the appearance of a relatively permissive copyright policy. I would argue instead that the process is highly exploitative and represents an extreme curtailing of expressive agency. The functioning of Content ID makes it possible not only for rightsholders to prohibit transformative expressions that copyright law may well deem fair, but also to commercially exploit them (sharing the profit with YouTube). As Sag notes, to subject copyright-related fairness determinations to monetization efforts "places a burden on expression and creativity" (2017, 558), in a way that undermines the ideals and objectives of the law. YouTube's algorithmic copyright adjudication tool is therefore designed not with the goal of facilitating the equitable enforcement of copyright law, but with that of maximizing monetization revenue. It does so by perpetuating a notion of singular, unified authorship that justifies the relegation of authorship and ownership claims from UGC creators to IP content owners. As such, Content ID represents a particularly powerful example of the impact AI can have at the intersection of agency and ownership.

A comparison to Adam Basanta's *All We'd Ever Need Is One Another* is again useful here. In the installation, the use of AI decenters authorial control and proposes a tongue-in-cheek deniability of human agency. This can serve as a speculative defence against infringement allegations, and furthermore as an indication that the outputs of this art factory—and the outputs of the underlying posthumanist agential assemblage—resist assimilation into the property-oriented circuits that have come to structure the contemporary cultural landscape. The operational logic of Content ID signals the opposite, namely that the aim here is to maximize the efficiency of the commercial exploitation of propertized expressions. In the process, the AI-driven tool curtails human expressive agency.

Regarding Basanta's project, I have also argued that it undermines the temporal logic of copying (i.e., that a copy exists in a clear before-after relationship with an original, from which it is derived), since the installation constitutes a sandboxed generative system that produces what could be described as copies without originals. Content ID, too, represents an intervention in the temporal logic of creative expression, but in this case, this occurs through a narrowing down, rather than opening up, of how creative expression is conceptualized and legitimized. Specifically, Content ID inverts the temporal logic of how infringement issues are dealt with: DRM systems such as this one can produce situations in which creative expressions are flagged and blocked before they appear online; situations, in other words, in which creative expressions are determined to infringe the copyright of other works before they can be perceived as such by human audiences. Content ID thus collapses the normal sequence of expression–complaint. Since YouTube itself could become liable for infringement complaints if it hosts unauthorized content, its filtering protocol operates predictively rather than reactively. This means that algorithmic DRM aims to adjudicate *ex ante*, i.e., before publication of the presumptively infringing content on the platform.[5] Fair use and fair dealing

5 See YouTube Help (n.d.): "Content ID continuously compares new uploads to the references for [the copyright owner's] assets. Matching videos are automatically claimed on behalf of the asset, and [the content owner's] specified match policy is applied to the claimed video before they are

exceptions, however, specify that the unauthorized use of a copyright-protected expression must be judged *ex post*, i.e., after the content has been published.

As I argued, *All We'd Ever Need Is One Another* problematizes whether a non-human-legible expression that remains sandboxed in a computational system can be meaningfully described as a "copy." Content ID goes a step further, and problematizes the ontology of "expression" itself: here, the algorithmically encoded assumption appears to be that perception through a human agent (rather than a DRM bot) is not necessary in order for an audio-visual artefact to infringe copyright. The problematic corollary of this is that established processes of dealing with infringement issues are fundamentally undermined, including the uploader's ability to defend their expression as fair after it has been published. (It is possible to appeal the decisions of Content ID; however, such appeals are initially deliberated in a para-legal sphere. For a layperson, it is exceedingly difficult to escalate such appeals to a court of law.) This interferes with the law's procedural logic of the fairness defence, and thus, again, with the enactment of expressive agency on behalf of the accused. While Basanta's art factory prevents publication of anything that does not match the digital fingerprints contained in its dataset of reference files, Content ID limits the externalization of everything that does. Or, put differently: *All We'd Ever Need Is One Another* provokes infringement allegations that are not easily justified; Content ID inverts this approach, and produces allegations that cannot easily be contested.

A system such as Content ID is built to enforce rules that are "simple to understand and enforce but lack nuance and

published on YouTube." (Note: 'match policy' refers to a content owner's registered preference regarding whether offending content should be monetized, blocked, or merely monitored.) On the topic of filtering before publication, see also Heldt 2019.

flexibility" (Burk 2019, 287). The copyright exceptions framed by the concepts of fair use and fair dealing, however, are meant to express complex legal norms and standards that are "flexible and context-sensitive but lack clarity" (ibid.). Without the nuance emphasized by Burk, it is practically impossible to defend the fairness of expressive activities that involve copyright-protected materials. The legal mechanisms by which the fairness of an unauthorized use of copyright-protected material are meant to be judged therefore cannot function according to the binary logic of right or wrong that is encoded into the analytical routines of Content ID (Edwards 2018, 68). Algorithmic adjudication, in this sense, "will drive a shift in norms toward 'codified' (that is, rule-driven) justice, as opposed to equitable justice" (Re and Solow-Niederman 2019, 246f.).

This kind of conceptual flattening has problematic implications for creative practices, and for the unencumbered digital circulation of information more generally. It would seem plainly obvious that creativity can never be evaluated according to a binary logic; and yet, systems such as Content ID are now controlling large swathes of the digital cultural landscape. With regard to issues of creative agency and cultural ownership, here the notion of "computational thinking" returns with a vengeance: instead of accommodating the complexities of expressive agency and the relationality of creativity, a gatekeeping system such as Content ID will shape how those it affects think of the processes it governs.[6]

6 Following Gillespie, Burk outlines a long list of problematic issues that run alongside these changed expectations, and which will inevitably arise in and through algorithmic copyright enforcement. Familiar from other studies on the self-reinforcing socio-economic impact of algorithmic bias, these include: the "illusion of objectivity," i.e., the assumption that the binding, quasi-legal determinations of the Content ID system do not involve human bias, which tends to create "the unwarranted perception of impartiality and objectivity;" "patterns of entanglement," i.e., the changing of user behaviors "under the influence of the algorithms they depend on;" and, perhaps most disturbingly, the "production of calculated publics," i.e., a self-reinforcing

Inevitably, individual agents will become habituated to the shifting functions and meanings of the law under this new, algorithmic copyright regime, with the result that the general understanding of permissible fairness exceptions—and, experientially, the nature both of creativity and of copyright law itself—will change, to the detriment of those whose expressive agency the law is meant to safeguard. Arguably, informed determinations concerning the permissibility of unauthorized creative expressions are effectively incomputable. In copyright contexts, the "ghost in the machine" of adjudication is the human ability to interpret creative expressions with nuance, and in all their relational complexity. Basanta's art factory foregrounds and highlights these crucial aspects of the new, speculative forms of creativity that posthumanist agential assemblages can make possible; Content ID, in turn, forecloses this possibility.

In combination, all of the issues outlined—Content ID's flattening of complex standards and norms into computable rules; its blackboxed and automated adjudication protocols; its reliance on *ex ante* presumptions of infringement; and its habituation of its subjects to its own decisions and decision-making processes—translate into a severe curtailing of human expressive agency. Content ID is therefore aligned, "materially through its computational procedures, economically through its monetization practices, and rhetorically through its published legal positions and community guidelines" (Edwards 2018, 62), with a restrictive and narrow perspective on expressive agency and ownership, which translates into a bias against the complexity of the kinds of relational creativity that fair use and fair dealing are meant to facilitate. Instead of framing dynamic and equitable engagement with creative expression, Content ID relegates control over it

pattern of interpretation, application, perception, and influence whereby the audience expectations *vis à vis* an algorithm and its behavior in response to the audience's behaviors are taken up more broadly throughout society (including by courts, policy-making bodies, etc.) and invade shared social and cultural norms as well as law and policy (Burk 2019, 285–95).

 to private arrangements that are codified and enforced in the shadow of the law.

What Content ID shares with *All We'd Ever Need Is One Another* is that both systems relegate the power of making determinations regarding the permissibility of digital expressions from the human to the non-human; what distinguishes them is that the purpose of this shift is reversed. *All We'd Ever Need Is One Another* invokes "similarity" to provocatively determine the artfulness of a digital artefact. Content ID, by contrast, will always consider similarity as an indication that the artefact under consideration is not eligible for the protection that copyright law offers for certain transformative copying activities. In Basanta's project, every non-match is deleted because it does not satisfy the similarity thresholds by which the system recognizes a generative output as a work of art. Content ID, in turn, permits only that which matches nothing, and in doing so it perpetuates an idealized romantic myth of the singularly original outputs of human creative genius. Here, similarity is indicative not of the relational and embedded nature of creative expression, but automatically of unlawful trespass on the enclosures of modern intellectual property. This is certainly not a posthumanist perspective on creativity, but, rather, one that dehumanizes creativity.

By contrast, the complex layering of generative and evaluative processes through which Basanta's art factory creates its outputs imply a posthumanist form of distributed creative agency that is embedded, dialogic, and relational in nature, and which may become incompatible with the conventional value propositions of contemporary IP regimes. But what does this mean for dehumanized IP-enforcement through DRM systems such as Content ID? Where algorithmic entities gain the power to police and curtail expressive agency, the loop between *Content ID* and *All We'd Ever Need Is One Another* closes. Basanta's project entangles human creativity with other, non-human agencies, such that the human participant(s) must relinquish authorial control; Content ID does not redistribute agency across multiple human and non-human entities, but only empowers a minimally-agential non-human system to judge expressions. The key difference is that while Content ID frames creativity through simplistic notions of originality that are derived from the humanist model of the artist and the artwork in order to further extend existing private property enclosures, Basanta's project implies a type of posthumanist agential assemblage that is no longer modelled anthropocentrically.

[7]

Toward a Becoming-Tactical of AI Art

At the outset of this book, I noted that the question of whether AI can be creative interests me only insofar as it represents an opportunity to rethink what "creativity" means in AI contexts, and how AI impacts issues of expressive agency and cultural ownership. In subsequent chapters, I discussed some examples of this impact, noting that even where AI becomes agential and presumptively creative, human agency persists. In my discussion of *Portrait of Edmond Belamy*, this has meant that non-human creativity is framed anthropocentrically and imagined as a "human-like" expressive agency somehow embodied in AI. In my discussion of Content ID, by contrast, it has meant that when an AI system is trained on narrowly conceived humanist notions of creativity, it cannot accommodate new kinds of expressive agency, but will instead perpetuate problematic ideals of unified, singular authorship. I have described these examples as strategic because they instrumentalize an anthropocentric conceptualization of creativity that sustains—or even amplifies—the economically motivated intellectual property (IP) models that characterize contemporary cultural landscapes. At the opposite end of the spectrum I have located tactical uses of AI, which disturb narrow conceptualizations of expressive agency and creativity instead of sustaining them. My main example of this has been that of Adam Basanta's art factory, in which agency is redistributed across multiple participating elements (human and non-human alike). I call such uses of AI tactical because they force a rethinking of what is meant by originality, authorship, and creative expression, of the political and aesthetic ideologies these concepts have traditionally relied upon, and of the socio-economic and legal regimes they serve. To round out my sketch of the becoming-tactical of AI in digital art practices, this chapter now brings into play a number of recent AI art projects that focus on the distributed nature of expressive agency in post-humanist agential assemblages.

I begin this discussion with *Machine Learning Porn* (2016) and *Zizi* (2019), two projects by the British artist Jake Elwes that enact a deliberate queering of AI and dataset politics. Both problematize the normative aspects of established perspectives on agency, with an explicit focus on sexual identity and an implicit focus on cultural ownership issues more generally. Following this, my final example is the Slovenian artist Maja Smrekar's ongoing project *!brute_force*, which introduces another form of intelligence to the interface between the human and AI. In *!brute_force*, canine intelligence becomes part of an experimental AI training regimen, in an effort to explore co-constitutive qualities of human and non-human knowledge ontologies. All of these projects go to considerable lengths to produce what I call posthumanist agential assemblages, featuring complexly entangled relational systems of decentered, co-constitutive, and intra-actional subject positions that reconfigure agency and cultural ownership beyond humanist, anthropocentric horizons.

Queering AI

Much of Jake Elwes' work engages critically with datasets and the politics around their compilation and use in AI contexts. As such, several of the artist's projects explore how queer subject positions and agential constellations can be framed by AI technology, but also what kinds of new constellation might emerge through such a framing. Regarding the practicalities of his approach, Elwes (2019b) has emphasized his strong interest in practices of appropriation. In the specific context of his work, this refers to the use of pre-existing datasets as well as pre-existing protocols of how neural networks interpret data for analytical and generative purposes. Elwes' appropriation-based approach differs from the methodologies of AI artists who favor the creation of original datasets, such as Anna Ridler or Helena Sarin. In an earlier chapter, I have suggested that artist-created datasets foreground the human element in computational creativity, something that can serve to perpetuate traditional notions of authorial control. Additionally, such approaches can reinscribe an anthropocentric framing of creativity expressed in the works, highlighting the human artist behind the work. The conceptual starting point for many of Elwes' projects is pitched differently. It resonates more closely with Crawford and Paglen's emphasis, in "Excavating AI" (2019b), on the importance of critiquing bias encoded in pre-existing data, rather than of reinscribing singular human agency in computational processes. In this sense, a basis for effective critique will involve existing bodies of data that can then undergo recalibration and reconfiguration, in ways which expose and challenge biases inherent either in the dataset itself or in the computational protocols to which it is subjected. This problematizes existing normative interactions between data, AI applications, and human agents.

Zizi, one of Elwes' most recent works, revolves around the AI-based generation of gender-fluid, androgynous drag portraits (fig. 7). In its first iteration, commissioned by Drew Hemment for the

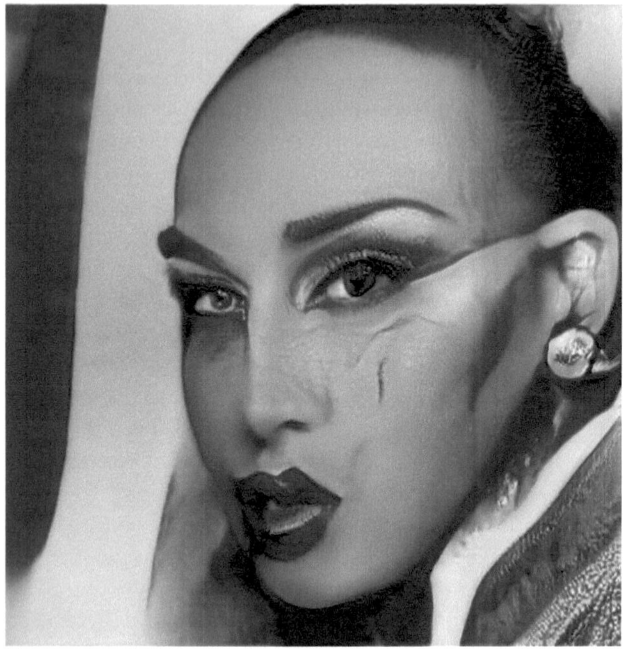

[Figure 7] Jake Elwes, *Zizi* (ongoing). Video still image used by permission of the artist.

Edinburgh-based *Experiential AI* initiative, the project offers a powerful critique of biased assumptions concerning gender identity that are encoded in training datasets commonly used for AI-based image-generation (see Elwes n.d.; Hemment 2019). Exhibited as a 135-minute video loop, *Zizi* features generative portraits of fictitious drag artists that continuously morph between recognizable faces and colorful abstraction. This output is achieved through the use of a pre-existing neural network using the StyleGAN architecture, which was trained on Nvidia's open source Flickr-Faces-HQ (FFHQ) dataset. The system was then re-trained on a new dataset of roughly 1,000 portraits of drag performers, which had been scraped from various websites and social media profiles. The resulting video footage produces an exhilarating impression of diversity and difference, while at the same time also conveying a sense of continuity and community across the generated portraits.

When AI generates realistic images of human-like faces, the training datasets that are used will inevitably prescribe a horizon of possibilities concerning the outputs, no matter how much the rhetoric framing of the system might wish to emphasize the "unpredictability" or "originality" of the generated images. (*Portrait of Edward Belamy*, discussed in chapter 4, is a case in point; because it draws on the art historical canon of classic portraiture, it embodies many familiar, staid conventions of the form, even though it was supposedly created anew by an artificial intelligence.) *Zizi* highlights this contradiction and challenges the appearance of difference that generative AI gives. The critical position projected by the work is that generative systems synthesizing "new" images of human faces actually tend to amplify existing biases and will likely exclude large demographics, simply based on the nature of the training data and the generative algorithms that are being used. It is only by injecting difference into the training data that *Zizi* can itself highlight the lack of diversity and representation in mainstream AI. As a critique of the spectularized "newness," "originality," or "creativity" of AI-generated outputs, *Zizi* suggests that dataset bias will in fact accentuate and perpetuate a normative sameness that is concealed beneath the problematic rhetoric veneer of AI-based, non-human expressive agency.

This message takes on an additional critical edge through the project's thematic focus on drag. Reminiscent of other GAN-style systems that can generate portraits of non-existent human figures, *Zizi* outwardly appears as a relatively straightforward image-synthesis tool. But in its speculative alignment between generative machine learning and drag, the project challenges the presumptive originality that is often assigned to AI-generated images. As a cultural form with an important critical dimension, drag itself draws powerfully on playful techniques of imitation, defamiliarization, and mimicry—techniques that can also be located in the functionality of GANs as described in earlier chapters. Drag's performance of difference and its underlying problematization of essentialist gender norms is partly based on copying practices, and highlights, as Judith Butler (1998) and many other since have noted, that gender itself is an imitation without an original. *Zizi* thus foregrounds a speculative alignment between drag and generative AI, but also emphasizes a key difference: while both drag and generative AI might appear to operate by way of amplifying stereotypes and accentuating difference, drag inherently challenges what generative AI reinforces. In the fictitious, morphing portraits *Zizi* generates, the "permanent becoming of a GAN" resonates with the "fluidity, ambiguity and transition of drag" (Hemment 2019). With regard to critical issues of agency and identity, however, the message leveraged through *Zizi* is that the posthumanist potential of AI-based expressive agency is not realized in the mainstream systems and datasets generally used for GAN-style image synthesis.

The 1,000 drag artist portraits used for retraining the mainstream AI system on which *Zizi* is based were scraped without seeking permission, which might raise some ethical concern. But I would argue that the artist's decision to proceed in this fashion underlines the conceptual integrity of the project. The appropriative gesture aligns with the formal and ideological approaches of drag itself; the use is non-exploitative and, in fact, critical of exploitation; and the appropriation functions as a reminder that extensive datasets used in many commercial applications—including the FFHQ dataset itself—tend to be based on the massive-scale unauthorized appropriation of private information.[1] As Elwes notes, none of the drag images that were

1 Note that for new iterations of *Zizi*, Elwes has been actively collaborating with drag performers (personal correspondence with the artist, May 24, 2020). One result of such collaboration, *The Zizi Show*, was released online in mid-March 2021.

used make direct reference to individuals, nor do the resulting outputs render specific drag performers recognizable. Rather, the approach produces a "queer amalgamation" that is intended to challenge the normative and exclusionary identity politics projected through the pre-existing network. In other words, the approach here is a tactical critique of an existing dataset based on the injection of disruptive elements, rather than the strategic exploitation of misappropriated training data. This entails a recalibration of the evaluative and generative processes critiqued in *Zizi*, a sort of repetition with a difference that exposes hetero-normative biases encoded in mainstream image datasets.

Again, this highlights how generative AI tools that are framed as capable of generating novel and original outputs may instead merely perpetuate objectionable attitudes encoded in the underlying training data, and, indeed, help to normalize these attitudes. This echoes an argument made earlier with regard to AI-based gatekeeper systems such as Content ID, which habituate users to norms encoded in and amplified through AI systems, rather than allowing users to attune to difference. In this sense, *Zizi* emphasizes the work that is required to ensure that mainstream networks do more than merely generate exclusionary sameness and disguise it as difference. In the project's appropriation of drag aesthetics and ethics, and in its injection of these into the FFHQ ecology, the repetition of training and generative processes does indeed produce radical difference.

One of Elwes' earlier projects, *Machine Learning Porn* (2016), follows a similar approach. Here, the open-sourced *open_nsfw* network, designed by the tech giant Yahoo to identify online image content that may be considered sexually explicit or offensive (including pornography, sexual violence, but also mere nudity), is reengineered so that the classifiers used for content recognition become parameters for generating image content (fig. 8). The resulting video output is unsettling and strange: it never fully resolves into anything entirely representational, but nevertheless conveys a vague "porn" quality that leads viewers

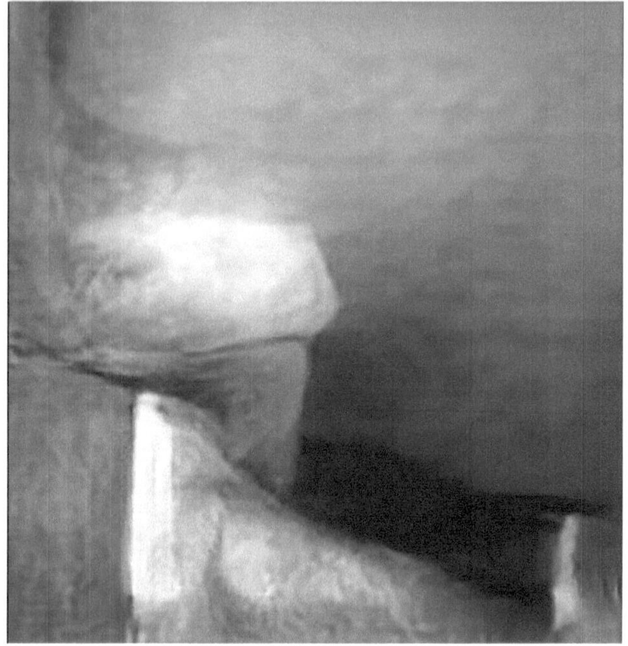

[Figure 8] Jake Elwes, *Machine Learning Porn* (2016). Video still image used by permission of the artist. (Video available at https://vimeo.com/213923669.)

to question the prejudices on which their own interpretations of "offensive" audio-visual content are based. Inevitably, this involves asking what norms for "inappropriate content" may be encoded in the underlying dataset, what algorithmic processes of habituation viewers are exposed to when they browse content that is pre-filtered by tools such as *open_nsfw*, and how the biases on which such filtering is based may ultimately become encoded in the viewers' own interpretive faculties. By turning a filtering system into a generative system, *Machine Learning Porn* pushes a neural network originally designed to censor images in a new direction, and coaxes it into transgressing normative boundaries of anatomy, gender, and sexual identity on which filtering networks may otherwise rely. *Machine Learning Porn* thus engenders a system that behaves "progressively" both because of and despite the biases of the underlying training data.

Like *Zizi*, *Machine Learning Porn* appropriates pre-existing neural networks and data. This includes an influential visualization technique developed by Ahn Nguyen et al. (2016) for the Evolving AI Laboratory, as well as experiments based on this technique, conducted by Gabriel Goh (n. d.; Vincent 2016).[2] A brief comparison between *Machine Learning Porn* and the operational logic of these mainstream AI experiments helps to clarify the becoming-tactical of AI that is evident in Elwes' project. Nguyen et al.'s underlying research focuses on the deveopment of ways to visualize momentary states of network neurons at any given moment during a learning/training procedure. Somewhat problematically, the project setup implies that machine learning "thought processes" are analogous to known human brain functionality, and that on the basis of this anthropocentric analogy, it is possible to objectively visualize diachronic snapshots of artificial neural network nodes. Gabriel Goh's subsequent work applied the earlier findings to Yahoo's open-sourced *open_nsfw* neural network. Using Nguyen et al.'s technique, Goh fine-tuned a system trained on the Yahoo dataset in order to investigate the specific thresholds used in Yahoo's filtering system for determining what characterizes a given image as "not safe for work." In the documentation for the project, Goh references the Yahoo project website's declaration that "Defining NSFW material is subjective" and that "what may be objectionable in one context can be suitable in another." But Goh's work does not take into account what strikes me as the most important implication of these statements, namely that *open_nsfw* encodes and reifies the biases of the Yahoo engineers and clickworkers who classified the training data. Instead, Goh uses the dataset to assign descriptors such as "clearly pornographic" or "only

2 Note that Goh's work, referenced in the following paragraphs, is no longer online. At the time of writing, a snapshot of the relevant page, including exemplary image material, is archived on Gwern Branwen's website.

 seemingly innocent" (emphasis in original) to the generative outputs of the newly created system.

As Goh puts it, "Once you see the true nature of these images ... it becomes impossible to unsee" (n. d.). It would seem to me that this assertion harbors a fundamental confusion regarding the nature of non-human expressive agency. The "true" nature of the generated outputs is, of course, inscribed through human-created labels in the dataset. In this sense, Goh fails to acknowledge that the system's outputs are variations of norms encoded in the underlying dataset. Biases and ideological frameworks inscribed in the training data and the classification system are thus ignored, and once more, the agential assemblage generating the images is itself framed anthropocentrically. Ultimately, the experimentation undertaken in Goh's project lacks criticality and is oriented toward the kind of technical mastery described by the concept of computational thinking. Other experiments at the intersection of AI and pornographic content share this orientation. On a Reddit thread devoted to the topic, many of the listed projects focus on the reverse engineering of commercial tools, but none of them aim to develop new, critical ways of seeing. Instead, virtually all of the listed projects endeavor to streamline the efficiency of consuming normatively classified pornographic content ("Machine Learning Porn").

In the framework I have established here, such experiments have to be described as strategic, and stand in stark contrast to the conceptual thrust of art works such as *Zizi* and *Machine Learning Porn*, which appropriate and redeploy existing technologies in order first to point at the problematic anthropocentric norms inscribed in them, and then to push beyond these. Elwes' work adopts existing registers of sexual identity politics and technological protocols of biased data evaluation only in order to subject all of this to a tactical queering. AI is thus speculatively pushed into a sphere of posthumanist expressive agency that may reflect back some of the anthropocentric distortions, exclusions, and exploitations effected through the technology, but which does not perpetuate them.

New Vectors of Non-Brute Force Computation

Slovenian artist Maja Smrekar's ongoing AI project *!brute_force*, which intersects digital art, behavioral psychology, and AI development, moves in a similar direction. Here, a series of ludo-scientific experiments that involve humans, dogs, and AI-based participants aid in a speculative rethinking of the co-constitutive and co-determinative nature of different agential entities and the subject positions they inhabit. *!brute_force* revolves around iterative interactions of the project participants within a three-dimensional sculptural grid consisting of movable panels (fig. 9). A human and a dog are guided by an AI system in traversing the structure, while also responding to the behaviors of one another and producing data that informs further computational processes. All of the participants represent performers as much as test subjects, evaluative tools as much as training data sources. They are networked with the aim of distributing agential attributes and characteristics across them. The grid is modelled on the molecular structure of serotonin, a human neurotransmitter associated with the feeling of well-being and happiness, whose metabolic function has been crucially shaped by the co-evolution of human and dog. In each iteration of the project, the AI system—a convolutional neural network, or CNN—guides the artist and her dog companion as they navigate the modular grid structure, with the uncertain ambition of creating a state of equilibrium across biometric diagnostic data collected from both participants (see fig. 10). The data collected in each iteration is evaluated by the AI system and used in reconfiguring the grid's layout for the following iteration. This open-ended feedback loop of co-determinative learning, training, and action crosses human/non-human boundaries, and invokes the inter-species, co-evolutionary development of the serotonin molecule itself.

!brute_force explores fundamental agential entanglements between the human, the canine, and AI, and rejects as humanist

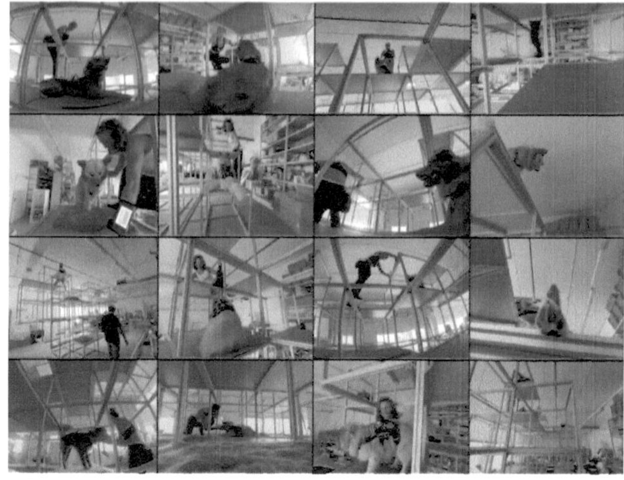

[Figure 9] Maja Smrekar, *!brute_force* (ongoing). Still image from video doumentation used by permission of the artist.

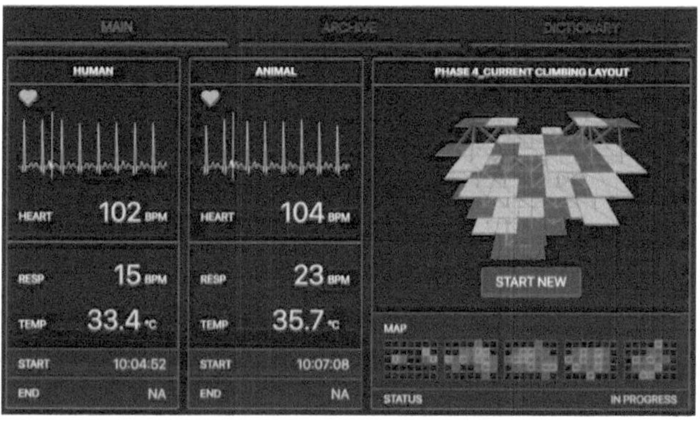

[Figure 10] Maja Smrekar, *!brute_force* (ongoing). Still image from video doumentation used by permission of the artist.

fantasy the centrality or supremacy of a presumptively singular, unified human agent. Beyond the revisionist notion of inter-species subjugation that is sometimes used to characterize the domesticated dog, the project asks whether non-human interactions can instead open up toward a new "symbiotic code" of posthumanist agency (Smrekar n.d.). In its iterative feedback cycles, *!brute_force* produces just such an agential assemblage, in which all elements co-determine and continuously refine new knowledge and training data for one another. The assemblage thus constituted does not feature a clear center, and the interactions and learning processes afforded by it produce new types of emancipatory, equitable, posthumanist relationships between the AI system, artist, and dog participants.

The iterative format of *!brute_force* is designed to invoke, but also to challenge conventional expectations regarding the products of art-making, research, and AI development. In this way, the project undermines humanist ideals of meaning-making that would dictate outcomes such as finished artworks, reproducible results from scientific experiments, or high-efficiency machine learning algorithms. What the entanglements between the project participants in *!briute_force* develop instead is a more open-ended cognitive mode through which boundaries between human agency and its computational and animal others can be redrawn. Notably, this is done not in order to augment the human, but instead to better understand how human agency is always dynamically co-determined by and through its interactants. When the participants navigate the iteratively reconfigured grid structure, what emerges is a cognitive vocabulary of co-contingent subjectivity and action that is shared across the entire agential assemblage.

As Smrekar notes, creating such a vocabulary "is not a suggestion for improving the algorithm, as it usually is the case in automated procedures within machine learning, it rather addresses the constructs of ideological markers that (re)shape our cognitive reality" ("Towards the Final Concept Frame"). Crucially, this vectorization of agency manifests not only in a dog's ability to navigate the grid calculated for it by the AI system, but simultaneously in the human ability to build the structure, and in the ability of the AI system to remodel the grid designs based on its observation of the project participants' interaction with them. In this sense, the central question that drove *!brute_force* when Smrekar began to develop the project—"What Can Artificial Intelligence Learn from Dogs?"—now appears as a bit of a ruse: while the question invokes conventional machine learning aims of perfecting prediction algorithms, the project methodology actually contradicts the conventional approaches this would imply. In their place, other, more interesting questions arise. What could AI learn about humans from the ways in which they have sought to shape canine agency over time? How could humans use AI to better understand, in a self-reflexive mode, the co-contingent emergence of human and canine agency? How are these various training and learning modalities encoded in (and expressed through) the histories of dog training and the work now done to train AI?

A key conceptual point of departure for *!brute_force* is that technological infrastructures have always been linked to "a plethora of nonhuman actors," such as entanglements with weather, rocks, fungi, and so on (Smrekar, "What Can Artificial Intelligence Learn from Dogs?"). Based on the manifold presences of non-human actors in the ontological universe constructed and inhabited by human intelligence, Smrekar proposes that human actors need to "include non-human agency into the frame of re-thinking our place in the world, while addressing the question of where our technologies will take us in the future" (ibid.). To do so could mean, for example, to develop new posthumanist ontologies of affect, immediacy, and immanence—i.e., new modes of knowing and being that emerge from diagnostic, evaluative, and generative feedback cycles such as those afforded by *!brute_force*. Such ontologies bear markers of the tactical, rather than the strategic: they do not lend themselves well to the order of unified, singular subject positions, nor to the cultural ownership models or property regimes that rely on such subject positions.

This becomes evident in the project's appropriation-based approach to data collection and evaluation. When navigating the grid structure, both the artist and her dog collaborator wear customized electronical devices that record biometric data such as heartbeat and body temperature. These devices are hacked versions of commercially available electronic fitness trackers. The data they collect feeds into an archive maintained for the project itself, but also into the cloud-based storage system Apple Inc. uses for its mass-scale analysis of customer-supplied biometric data. As such, the collected data serves a double purpose. The first one, as already noted, is to provide training data for the *!brute_force* convolutional neural network, which then goes on to compute further iterations of the serotonin-based grid structure for the project participants to navigate. The second purpose is to infiltrate Apple Inc.'s proprietary health data ecology, in a speculative extension of the co-evolutionary transformations effected on and by the serotonin neurotransmitter. Because the hacked fitness tracker devices used in the project maintain an uplink to Apple Health, biometrical "data gathered from the dog's body gets routinely processed within the Apple cloud," where it represents a "disruption of the corporate statistics of human health" (Smrekar 2020). It is, of course, impossible to know how these rogue data uploads will be interpreted, or what effects they may have on the system. The injection of canine biometric information into Apple Inc.'s massive-scale, blackboxed mining operation of human-scraped health data is nonetheless a compelling tactical intervention. It highlights that digital health data analytics is not merely about health or well-being, but also raises important issues concerning ethics and privacy issues surrounding the collection and evaluation of such data.

In the current cloud-based, corporate-controlled information ecology, the data politics of Apple Health and similar services also entail strict IP enclosures that are being established whenever individuals agree to use health tracking services. Both the amount of relevant health data stored in corporate data vaults and the worldwide saturation of proprietary tracking/data-mining devices is immense. The consequence is that massive collections of private biometric data held by Apple and other corporate tech giants now constitute datasets of immeasurable economic and biopolitical value. This has been demonstrated with great urgency during the COVID-19 pandemic: coronavirus track-and-trace apps developed by tech corporations appear to outperform similar efforts developed at the state level (cf. French et al. 2020). As Smrekar (2020) notes, the first wave of the pandemic swept across Europe while *!brute_force* was in development; it was in this context that the emphasis on the politics and economics of health data took on a more important role in the project. Mass-marketed diagnostic wearables and the AI-based health monitoring technologies that operate in the background relate to highly sensitive personal information in extremely problematic ways. Who, Smrekar asks, will develop and control health communication protocols, who "will own our health data and who will have access to it?" (2020). These concerns regarding data privacy and the massive-scale commercial exploitation of users' health data point exactly to the agency and ownership issues that I have sought to highlight throughout this book.

!brute_force explores how new agential figurations challenge the teleological, predictive, and property-oriented ontologies of human agency as it has been traditionally conceived, and as it is now encoded and amplified in the computational sphere. The project's title is informative here: in programming, "brute force" refers to the solving of a problem through sheer computing power, while many programming languages use "!" as an operator signifying "not equal." The canine-human-computational assemblage that *!brute_force* constitutes thus speculates on a new, posthumanist agency of a "non-brute force" type. As Smrekar notes, contemporary views on AI continue to impose "our" understanding of human thinking processes onto non-human contexts. In this sense, "brute force computation" refers, first and foremost, to the strategy of eradicating a problem through

large-scale, top-down instrumentalization of a particular type of cognitive process. A frequently invoked example of this approach is the victory of the Deep Blue chess computer over Garry Kasparov in 1996, in which the human player was overpowered by the computer's ability to predict and evaluate every possible move including all of its possible consequences.

But similar effects can also be identified in other, seemingly more equitable approaches to advanced computation and artificial intelligence. An example of this is the astonishing success of the AlphaGo project, in which DeepMind Technologies (now owned by Google) developed an entirely self-taught AI system capable of beating the world's highest-ranked player of Go. The ancient board game of Go has far fewer rules than chess and affords the player more freedom to choose how to proceed through the game. It is, for these reasons, much more difficult to master than chess. The complexity of the game is such that the calculation and evaluation of all possible combinations of moves is technically impossible. While Deep Blue demonstrated that a game of chess can be won following a brute force strategy, it was until recently assumed that playing Go requires a more tactical approach, of which AI systems were considered to be incapable. When AlphaGo beat Lee Sedon in 2016, the event was widely hailed as a huge milestone for a type of next-wave AI technology that is immensely powerful, and additionally also described as a fundamentally accessible technology because it follows from-the-ground-up (rather than top-down) training methods (this view is still espoused by many; cf. du Sautoy 2019 and Miller 2019). It must be recognized, however, that achievements such as these are in fact not possible without the extreme consolidation and centralization of privately-owned resources and processing power. In various guises, the "master/slave" framework underlying strategic brute force computation therefore continues to ripple outwards from simple hardware contexts to the complex socio-economic, cultural, political, and philosophical issues of infrastructure ownership, inequitable power dynamics, privacy, access to knowledge and, ultimately, agency.

For now, the development of ever-more powerful AI technologies continues to take the form of self-reinforcing feedback loops in which the very idea of artificial intelligence circulates anthropocentrically, in the form of attempts to (re-)produce and control the activities and agential processes of human-like thinking machines.[3] In such contexts, the development of any presumptively non-human agency still hinges on brute force ideologies and imaginaries, in which power, control, and ownership are of central importance. *!brute_force*, by contrast, explores cognitive and computational vectors that gesture toward the co-determinative, symbiotic processes through which the affective and agential capabilities of human and dog were shaped. It is plainly evident how these diverge from the exploitation of clickworker labor, the blackboxing of proprietary predictive algorithms, or the massive-scale mining of private data, but also from the ways in which AI as such remains modelled on anthropocentric notions of intelligence and expressive agency.

In my reading, one of the key propositions of Smrekar's project is that just like the brute force training methods to which dogs have at times been subjected, the iterative reward-based feedback cycles on which contemporary machine learning conventionally relies can never hope to achieve more than transposing a reductive humanist ideal of agency to non-human contexts. *!brute_force* imagines a system that draws on something other than the centralized power structures dominating humanist thinking and being, in order to then facilitate the emergence of something other than anthropocentric notions of agency. The

3 Here, it is useful to acknowledge the etymology of "computer" as denoting a human agent who performs computational activities. For critical and artistic commentary on this, see Grier 2005, and also the American artist Jeff Thompson's project *Human Computers* (2020).

radical speculative thesis of the project is thus that the very concept of agency must reshape itself when it opens up to non-human subjectivities that are characterized by emancipatory qualities. Early in the development of the project, Smrekar noticed that once a dog had mastered a task, in follow-up encounters it began to approach this task playfully, and thus less predictably and, in the logic of computational thinking, less successfully ("Canine Training Data"). It is virtually impossible to model this "dog factor" algorithmically; more importantly, it also represents an element of canine agency that contradicts revisionist fantasies of humanity's "top-down" domestication of the dog. The behavior is evocative of de Certeau's tactical cunning (see my discussion in chapter 2), and thus itself takes the form of a challenge to the statistical order of computational efficiency that often structures AI development.

Similar to AI, dogs have long served as a kind of canvas onto which humans have projected their various notions of intelligence, creativity, and agency, many of them anthropocentrically framed by and reified in relationships of presumed domination and control. In this sense, I interpret the perception of the dog as an intelligent agent at least partly as a narcissistic affirmation of the imagined supremacy of a kind of human agency that is expressed precisely in its efforts to mold non-human agencies. As Smrekar notes, "any strategy for living in today's world depends upon attention to the here and now, and not to the illusory promises of computational prediction" ("What Can Artificial Intelligence Learn from Dogs?"). What implications, one wonders, could insights emerging from a non-brute force human-dog-AI paradigm have for anthropocentric property regimes and their efforts to strategically subsume human agency, algorithmic entities, and live non-human subjectivities? Perhaps one provisional answer to this question lies in the tactical subversion of IP enclosures that the posthumanist agential assemblage of *!brute_force* performs on proprietary collections of human health data.

 Tactical approaches to AI critically re-engineer emerging technologies. In doing so they enable reflexive, exploratory, and transformative interventions in the ideological substrates that organize AI and machine learning today. In the examples I have discussed, this has meant exploring the existing and emerging politics of complicated overlaps between agency and ownership in AI contexts, and resisting the assimilation of AI into regimes of capital, surveillance, and exploitative forms of algorithmic governmentality. Tactical uses of AI feed into opposition to such regimes, or can help, at least, to create speculative frameworks that make it possible to imagine such opposition. Rather than using AI merely as an aesthetic tool, tactical approaches explore and reconfigure what the technology itself is capable of hacking.

Where strategic AI hacks and disables the potential for radically new forms of distributed, posthumanist agential assemblages to emerge, tactical AI opposes the blackboxing of technology, its financialization and propertization, and any anthropocentric framing that continues to insist on elevating the human author-*qua*-owner above those non-human agencies with which is entangled. *!brute_force* encapsulates these qualities: it is inclusive, public-facing, and expansive, rather than exclusive, private, and restrictive. It appropriates and rethinks AI both at the level of the apparatus (algorithm, infrastructure) and at the level of the corpus (data). In this case, the becoming-tactical of AI in digital art points toward an "artistic intervention in the digital public sphere" (Smrekar 2020), or what I will call, in the last chapter, a posthumanist commoning of AI.

[8]

AI Art for a Posthumanist Cultural Commons

From the co-constitutive human-AI-canine knowledge ontologies envisioned in *!brute_force* to the defamiliarizing appropriation of AI functionality in *Zizi*, from the legal provocations of *All We'd Ever Need Is One Another* to the clumsy declamations of non-human creative agency in *Portrait of Edmond Belamy*, and from the uncloaking of AI bias in *ImageNet Roulette* to the problematic enactment of human non-agency in the Content ID system—what commonalities, productive contradictions, and critical potentialities reverberate across the examples discussed in the preceding chapters?

Throughout this book, I have considered my examples in relation to new kinds of agential assemblages that involve human and computational actants alongside one another. I identified agency and ownership as key concepts in exploring why such agential assemblages matter, what sort of meanings they create in contemporary socio-cultural landscapes, and how they can disturb existing anthropocentric paradigms of creative expression. As I have argued, agency and ownership are so important for this discussion in part because these concepts link together the entangled aesthetic, philosophical, legal, and socio-economic foundations underpinning the intellectual property (IP) enclosures of digital cultural landscapes. When AI manifests alongside its presumptively singular, individualized, and unified human counterparts in what I have called posthumanist agential assemblages, these enclosures lose their footing. And when a critical art of AI engages this development tactically, it has the potential to drive a radical decentering, redistribution, and recalibration of agency, such that humanist perspectives on creative expression, anthropocentric ideals of creativity, or restrictive views on human-only authorship may become unviable. One speculative consequence of this development is that ownership models which feed on these perspectives can themselves become subject to AI-driven critiques that undermine the cultural logic of IP.

What remains is to consider in more detail what sort of conceptual space is constituted by the becoming-tactical of AI in digital art projects. What are the critical stakes and implications of pushing past the ontological frameworks within which the artwork, the author, and the owner have traditionally circulated? What sort of political project is invoked when a critical art of AI speculates on the emergence of a new discursive matrix, a new environment—really: a new ecology—that manifests in and through the posthumanist agential assemblage as I have described it?

Having argued throughout that AI art can challenge anthropocentric perspectives both of the kind of agency conventionally required for creative expression, and of the ownership models that control the circulation of such expressions, this chapter rounds out my larger project with some thoughts on the possible critical trajectory implied in the becoming-tactical of AI. To do so, I follow a few strands from earlier chapters: I begin with a brief elaboration on my earlier discussion of GAN-style machine learning and GAN-based AI art. In that context, I revisit the problem of AI creativity in relation to IP frameworks, and expand on my suggestion that certain outputs of presumptively agential AI can be fundamentally incompatible with anthropocentric perspectives on creativity, originality, and authorship. Because such outputs resist assimilation into the property-oriented ownership models espoused by copyright, some recent scholarship suggests that they should be automatically relegated to the public domain. A short critique of this perspective will then bring me to the final part of my argument. The disturbances caused by AI with regard to agency and ownership call for more than merely the relegation of AI outputs to the insecure cultural commons of the public domain, which is, in effect, just another resource pool for further private property enclosures: what is needed instead is a posthumanist cultural commons that is co-constituted and co-determined—in a spirit of unownability rather than of property-to-be—by the works and the workings of the posthumanist agential assemblage.

GANs as "Generative Adversarial Copy Machines"

Artificial intelligence, I suggested in chapter 4, is a useful tool for challenging anthropocentric notions of what it means to create, to author, and to own. But this capability is not always realized tactically. My main example of this has been the GAN-style AI artwork *Portrait of Edmond Belamy*, which instrumentalizes AI strategically. As I argued, the work embodies a notion of AI creativity in which the humanist author figure and their creative genius are simulated computationally, and which aligns with anthropocentric ownership models. There is no consideration of the critical potential that may be enacted by new types of posthumanist expressive agency constituted in and through AI (unless one is inclined to accept spectacular claims of a "disruption of the art market" as such a potential). GAN functionality relies fundamentally on pre-existing data, from which it appears to "learn," and on the basis of which it can project the appearance of being capable of approximating (or even exceeding) human abilities of creative expression. In digital art contexts, descriptions of the technology tend to convey this through the rhetoric of art forgers trying to fool interlocutors into believing that their "fakes" and "copies" are "real" and "original" (cf. Sarin 2018; Ridler 2020; discussed in Zeilinger 2021). And yet, there is no doubt that the outputs of GAN systems can indeed be novel, and that they satisfy many conventional criteria of anthropocentrically framed creativity and originality. While such outputs may appear to successfully transpose aspects of human-style creativity to AI, they therefore also contradict humanist conceptions of creativity. Based on this paradox, in my discussion of *Portrait of Edmond Belamy* I argued that GAN systems synthesize new kinds of "copies without originals," which cannot be meaningfully described as reproductions of training data.

The members of Obvious Collective did not seem to see themselves as participants of a posthumanist agential assemblage. Situating *Portrait of Edmond Belamy* as a valuable and unique aesthetic artefact, they instead proposed that conventional views on creativity, originality, and ownership models can persist in AI art. When it became clear that the collective's appropriation of Robbie Barrat's underlying work in fact violated these same views, from a conceptual standpoint their proposition fell apart. In elaborating on this argument, I want to suggest that to use GAN systems tactically is to foreground—rather than obfuscate – the relational entanglements between human and non-human participants, between existing expression and generative novelty. Here, GANs become "generative adversarial copy machines," rather than tools that are idealistically and naively framed as approximations of human creativity even when their outputs ultimately appear unimaginative and rather expectable.

In technical terms, it is clear that a GAN system iterates over training data until it can reliably surpass the threshold at which the Generator's outputs convince the Discriminator that a generative "fake" is, in fact, a "real" original. GAN "creativity," it follows, works within an horizon of originality that is fundamentally anchored in repetition. Some current views ignore this and instead proceed along a different human-AI analogy: in recent publications by du Sautoy (2019) and Miller (2019), for example, the yardstick for measuring AI creativity is, once again, the art-historical manifestation of the romantic artist figure and its creative genius capable of producing unique aesthetic artefacts. Against this perspective, I would argue that in AI contexts, such outputs, no matter how compellingly they might appear to approximate anthropocentric norms of creative originality, are better described as a new kind of Baudrillardian simulacra.

To spin this thought further: if GAN outputs—framed as artworks—constitute copies without originals, then GAN systems—viewed as agential assemblages with expressive capabilities—resemble bodies without organs. Katherine Hayles (1999), Patricia Pisters (in Braidotti and Hlavajova 2018) and others have pointed out that this concept, borrowed from Antonin Artaud and popularized by Gilles Deleuze and Félix Guattari, is useful for critiquing the Enlightenment notion of autonomous subjectivity. In the given context, I would argue that the workings of a GAN system itself can constitute just such a critique: the "adversarial" interplay (or intra-action) between Generator and Discriminator may appear to project a kind of split personality, a simple competitive duality revolving around "copy" and "original," "fake" and "real;" but more importantly, it also represents a decentered agential assemblage that will not and cannot conform to the conventions by which the unified agency of the humanist artist figure has traditionally been identified. A GAN system engaged in presumptively creative processes that might be interpreted as capable of yielding novel, unique, and original aesthetic artefacts thus also always represents "wider distributions of agency," to use Jane Bennet's (2009, 122) formulation, across the porous boundaries of the AI system's co-constitutive generative elements.

These distributions, in my view, extend beyond a GAN system's computational components, and manifest as "mutual constitutions of entangled agencies" (Barad 2007, 33) that integrate computational and algorithmic components with their human designers, programmers, owners or operators, and likewise with the information, biases, and subjectivities expressed in training data sets. In this view, the entanglements that characterize GAN-style AI art can be seen to result in expressive outputs and behaviors that are not likely to align with how agency is conceived in and through humanist paradigms of creativity, originality, and authorship, nor, again, with the ownership models underpinned by these.

Joanna Zylinska recently commented that "much of current AI art, especially of the computer- and data-based kind, ends up generating an odd combination of the fuzzy, the mindless and the bland" (2020, 72). Yet GAN-style AI is perhaps not quite as dumb, boring, predictable, or meaningless as it can appear to be. Yes, easy analogies between surprising, novel GAN outputs and the traditional notion of the unknowable creative genius of human artists are shallow and trite. But in any case, neither the expressive "minds" of AI systems nor the expressions they are capable of producing are ultimately consistent with the romantic model of singular expressive agency that AI art is popularly meant to invoke. Instead, such systems align much more closely with the ways in which posthumanist thought conceptualizes agency. Artificially intelligent agential assemblages here emerge as decentered and relational, rather than as internally unified and singular. "Creativity" now can no longer be argued to work from the blank slate of pure inspiration (as if it ever had); rather, in the ways in which it manifests in GAN outputs it becomes another reminder that this blank slate does not, in fact, exist. Operating as relational systems, GANs have become embedded in cultural and technological ecologies, which they access through training data and the subjectivities inscribed through human agents who are inevitably involved in the generative processes that an AI system may be capable of.

It might be objected that the notion of relationality does not map smoothly onto AI. In Craig and Kerr's writing on the (im)possibility of AI authorship (discussed in depth in chapter 3), the authors note that the same characteristics which render authorship relational and dialogic also require the recognition of authorship as a "communicative act that is inherently social," which is marked by a "cultivation of selfhood" (2021, 44) not accessible to AI. But approaching the expressive agency of AI through a posthumanist framework allows for relational and dialogic processes to become decoupled from an anthropocentric focus of human-only social and communicative interactions (and also from human-only-made artefacts), so that relationality can persist in entanglements in which both human and non-human agential entities participate. The point of insisting on this distinction is that the disaggregated expressive agency of artificial intelligence, when it is framed in this way, ultimately aligns more closely with exactly the kind of progressive view on a human creativity of the dialogic/situated self through which critics of the romantic author figure have long sought to disrupt narrow conceptions of authorship and ownership. As Karen Barad notes with regard to the specific example of writing, such expressive activity represents "an iterative and mutually constitutive working out, and reworking, of 'book' and 'author'" (2007, x). Applied to the use of GAN-style AI systems for creative expression, this observation can surely be read as suggesting that critical uses of AI are capable of achieving something other than merely an imitative approximation of human creativity.

My argument, ultimately, is that even when GAN-style AI art tends to be evaluated based on how effectively it embodies the "external hallmarks of human creativity" (Craig and Kerr 2021, 73), it also structurally undermines the ontological and conceptual integrity of that idea of creativity. In conjunction with the qualities of relationality and decenteredness that I have identified in the speculative expressive agency of GANs, this means that when AI art destabilizes the concept of the human artist figure, it cannot likely replace this subject position by another unified (non-human) author. This has serious critical implications not only for the aesthetic interpretation of AI art, but also for socio-economic perspectives on originality, the AI art author figure, and the legal status of the AI artwork itself.

AI Beyond the Public Domain

My discussion of the potential for AI creativity in chapter 3 cast doubt on the extent to which the expressions of a posthumanist agential assemblage could be accommodated within legal frameworks that rely on humanist, anthropocentric notions of authorship. Some of the theoretical perspectives I introduced as part of that discussion challenge the notion that AI outputs can be defined as human-authored expressions; other critical voices insist that AI cannot be properly recognized as having "authored" its outputs. Given these concerns, what framework of cultural or legal ownership could accommodate the outputs of expressive AI?

Some recent legal scholarship proposes that AI outputs cannot seem to satisfy the legal requirements necessary to qualify for copyright protection. The logic underlying this suggestion implies that if human agents cannot legitimately claim authorship of AI-generated works, and if an AI system itself cannot be granted the agency required for it to qualify as an author figure and/or owner of IP rights, then such outputs must be placed in the public domain, where they would become freely available as a common source of inspiration for further human-authored creative expression.

Sarit Mizrahi, for example, offers a comprehensive discussion of quasi-autonomous AI and robotic outputs and suggests the inclusion of such works in the public domain as the only sensible approach, for the simple reason that current copyright legislation does not apply to "faux-riginal" (2019) works. Ana Ramalho (2017) arrives at a similar conclusion, on the basis of arguing that AI-generated outputs, for all intents and purposes, are in fact authorless. What these insightful essays do not consider in enough depth is whether the automatic placing of AI outputs into the public domain can become the foundation for a radically new perspective on the interfacing of AI and IP. It would appear, after all, that such a move situates AI-generated expressions outside the immediate reach of many of the privatization and propertization effects that are otherwise immediately imposed by contemporary IP regimes. But this potential remains unexplored in these examples; both Mizrahi and Ramalho structure their arguments as pragmatic responses to current limitations of IP law with regard to AI copyrightability.

In the most general sense, the public domain is conceived as a conceptual sphere containing creative works that are not covered by exclusive IP rights. This may be because such rights were waived, have expired, or simply because no such rights apply to the works in question. This does not mean, however, that materials contained in the public domain cannot become someone's private property. In the utilitarian logic of IP, the public domain is seen as a resource pool of freely accessible materials out of which authors-to-be can appropriate source materials, which will then, as new expressions, once again be subject to the access and use restrictions stipulated by IP law. The public domain, in other words, is a legal construct that exists alongside a framework of private intellectual property enclosures rather than outside it. It may draw its contents from these enclosures, but it simultaneously also feeds into them.

The public domain thus both parallels and precedes property enclosures. Some of the arguments formulated in John Locke's *Two Treatises on Government* (1690), frequently invoked when political theory, philosophy, or legal theory debate the origins and teleology of the private property enclosures facilitated by IP law, are a good example of this. According to Locke, property arises out of that which "Nature hath provided" (§26), i.e., that which is contained in a vaguely delineated commons. As Locke famously proposed, "every man has a 'property' in his own person," and therefore also in the "labour of his body, and the work of his hands" (ibid.); from this, it follows that by mixing one's labor with anything sourced from the commons, private property can be appropriated from this commons. This logic lends itself well for expansion into the realm of creative expression. Peter Jaszi is among many legal theorists who have elaborated how Locke's labor theory of property "at least implicitly identified the individual's proprietorship over himself as a function of 'authorship'" (1991, 470). Reference to Locke's theory is thus found throughout early authorship disputes and copyright statutes, where it was drawn upon both for legitimizing and for critiquing the notion that authors are owners, but also for conceptualizing the vaguely defined cultural commons that became the public domain (see, for example, Rose 1995; Boyle 2008).

Let me return to the question of whether AI works should be placed in the public domain. It is clear that such a move could have dramatic consequences. In economic terms, it would mean that the monetary value bound in AI works might escape immediate capture through some of the corporate entities that drive AI development. In more philosophical terms, the automatic placing of AI works in the public domain could also imply an in-principle disavowal of the possibility that AI can be granted authorial agency or personhood, even if its behaviors, abilities, and outputs were to match (or exceed) the definitional thresholds by which human creativity is conventionally determined. According to du Sautoy (2019) and others who emphasize the effective computability of creativity, it seems inevitable that AI will develop in that direction; but from a legal perspective, even works that perfectly resemble creative, original, authored works would currently have to be denied recognition as such. Assuming that AI will continue to inch in the general direction of

"AI-completeness," and that the human capacity to distinguish between AI-generated and human-generated works will continue to diminish, a decision to exclude AI works from the purview of copyright as a matter of principle would end up contradicting (and potentially invalidating) established juridical baselines for defining and determining copyrightability more generally. This, I would argue, is the radical implication of the automatic relegation of AI works to the public domain.

Neither Mizrahi nor Ramalho frame their proposition to place AI works in the public domain as a gesture towards disturbing or disrupting the ownership models facilitated by the logic of IP. The points they raise are nevertheless important, since they highlight the significant economic values that are now embodied in AI-generated outputs. What Mizrahi and Ramalho clearly imply is that society at large could derive immense benefit if AI works were to become freely accessible for further use. However, given the fact that ready-made and far-reaching legal regulation—such as that offered by copyright law—already exists, it is highly unlikely that the economic values represented by AI-generated outputs will be relinquished in this way. What the history of expansive, overbearing IP suggests instead is that established frameworks are much more likely to be reconfigured only to such a degree that AI works can be comfortably assimilated into existing regimes, most likely as human-authored works, and they will thus remain subject to already-existing IP rights. This assumption can also be inferred from Craig and Kerr's observations. The more likely it is that AI outputs are perceived, from an aesthetic perspective, as creative, the less likely it is that in economic contexts they will be perceived as authorless. Once again, "the romantic author can be seen racing into action—as it has, historically—in service of economic interests and the continued expansion of copyright's domain" (Craig and Kerr 2021, 73).

Perhaps the fact that Mizrahi and Ramalho do not explore the disruptive potential of their proposal to put AI works in the public domain can be read as cautionary pragmatism. I remain unconvinced, in any case, that the public domain is an appropriate vehicle to counteract the restrictive enclosures of IP. In Locke's labor theory of property, the commons is understood as a sphere of public (or shared) property that facilitates the engendering of private property. Within the broader context of contemporary IP regimes, the value of the public domain in this sense consists precisely in its intimate connection to the ownership models that it ultimately helps to sustain by providing freely accessible materials as the basis for further enclosures. The public domain, then, does not strike me as a viable ecology for accommodating the works of posthumanist agential assemblages, in part because it effectively frames its contents for assimilation into the anthropocentric IP enclosures into which it feeds. A more radical gesture would be to place the works of the posthumanist agential assemblage not in a context of "becoming-IP," but instead in a context that might better accommodate its speculative quality of what I have earlier described as unownability.

Unownability in the Posthumanist Cultural Commons

Following the trajectory of my arguments throughout this book, what the emergence of the posthumanist agential assemblage calls for is not a public domain for AI works, but instead a more fundamental rethinking of the commons for posthumanist contexts. A key question that such a rethinking needs to be able to answer is what sort of commons can accommodate such works beyond the reach of intellectual property enclosures. Where and how can a critical art of AI that contests humanist notions of agency and ownership, as well as the underpinning Enlightenment values of the centrality, singularity, and supremacy of the human artist/author figure, be contained? In what conceptual space, and by what aesthetic, philosophical, ethical, ideological, or legal frameworks could such containment be delineated?

As noted, the public domain was itself conceived as a kind of cultural commons, a concept that predates the appearance of IP enclosures by several centuries.[1] Lewis Hyde, a wonderfully eloquent and insightful thinker on the general subject, uses the terms more or less interchangeably (e.g., Hyde 2010); the IP theorist James Boyle, similarly, discusses the public domain in relation to a "commons of the mind" (2008). But continuities across the two concepts also mean that the cultural commons itself is subject to some of the same criticisms outlined above concerning the public domain. In Locke's labor theory of property, for example, the commons appears as what Hyde calls a rather implausible "primordial state" (2010, 20) that implies not only the centrality and supremacy of the human, but which also invokes colonialist ideologies (Locke himself reportedly wrote the *Second Treatise on Government* with "America" in mind). In the influential writing of the English jurist Sir William Blackstone (1723–1780), the commons was similarly conceptualized as an "immediate gift of the Creator," from which everyone can take "to his own use such things as his immediate necessities required" (Morrison 2001). Notably, both Locke and Blackstone invoke the commons in direct relationship to ownership: the commons is the "general property of mankind," writes Blackstone, and as such it serves as a resource pool for the kinds of appropriation which, following Locke, engender private property. This framing of the commons as a type of (non-private) preternatural property enclosure persists; it is still evident in how the public domain is conceptualized, and has helped determine the organization of most contemporary cultural commons (including the Creative

1 The first explicitly framed enclosures of cultural commons are generally traced to the granting of privileges to printers in mid-15th century Venice (see, for example, Hyde 2010); in legal history, Great Britain's *Statute of Anne* (1710) is considered one of the first copyright statutes of note. This statute also encoded explicitly the concept of terminal copyright protection as well as the notion of a public domain into which works, once out of copyright, were to be placed.

 Commons initiative, as well as various communities in the Free and Open-Source Software [FOSS] movement).

But Blackstone goes beyond describing the commons as a source from which private property enclosures arise. He also sees it as a sphere that belongs to humankind "exclusive of other beings." This reaffirms again that the commons itself resembles an abstract property enclosure, and also means that the concept assumes both the unified, singular nature of the human subject who is entitled to exploit it, and the centrality of this human subject. The commons, in other words, exists for the benefit of the human agent (and the communities or collectives of which it may be a member), but at the expense of every other non-human system within which the human itself may be embedded. The legal philosopher Merima Bruncevic (2018) is certainly correct in emphasizing that this anthropocentric perspective of the commons—as a sphere revolving around the human subject's exclusive privilege to appropriate from it articles of private property—is of questionable usefulness for any posthumanist project.

There are, of course, contemporary perspectives on the commons that branch off from the more traditional views just introduced. Michael Hardt and Antonio Negri, for example, work with a notion of the commons that "does not position humanity separate from nature, as either its exploiter or its custodian, but focuses rather on the practices of interaction, care, and cohabitation, in a common world, promoting the beneficial and limiting the detrimental forms of the common" (Hardt and Negri 2009, viii). In a comprehensive reframing of the commons within the domain of posthumanism, Bruncevic expands on this view to develop a perspective in which the commons is perceived as a fundamentally relational concept, rather than merely as a boundary-setting device that makes future property enclosures possible. Bruncevic defines the commons "as an ecology, as the in-between or the entanglement of personhood-property space" (122), which does not favor "clear divisions between physical/intellectual; between human/non-human; between commons/

commoneers" (145). Here, the commons contradicts not only anthropocentric hierarchies of human supremacy, but more generally any perspective that separates "the human from its environments and surroundings" (146).

Importantly, the existence of the commons as an "entanglement of personhood-property" highlights the agency of those who are (and of that which is) contained in the commons. This amplifies what is at least partly already implied in Hardt and Negri's vision of the commons: the non-human is now included not simply as part of the exploitable resource pool, but instead it becomes an integral part of a chorus of agencies that co-determine the existence, but also the functioning and safeguarding of the commons itself. The non-human, in other words, is no longer only object, but also subject of the commons.

How can such a commons accommodate the non-human beyond the natural, and extend itself to the works and workings of the posthumanist agential assemblage as I have described it? How can it take into account exteriorizations of the human that also include, in alignment with Bernard Stiegler's concept of "technics," computational technologies such as AI? Following on from criticisms of the public domain as a type of cultural commons that remains constricted through its connection to private property enclosures, I suggest that a posthumanist cultural commons must satisfy at least two requirements: it has to exist beyond assumptions of the centrality of human agency; and it must be able to withstand the immediate and constant threat of being assimilated into anthropocentric IP enclosures. It is certainly possible to theorize the formation of such a commons; what is more difficult is to imagine how it might be safeguarded through the types of legal frameworks that have historically been available.

Bruncevic, who, like me, formulates her definition of a posthumanist commons in relation to art and IP theory, draws on the concept of the hyperobject as a key tool in her discussion. Coined by the cultural philosopher and object-oriented ontology theorist Timothy Morton (2013), the concept is useful for discussing extremely complex phenomena (such as climate change) that defy pinpointing in time and space, and which are characteristically decentered as well as massively distributed. As Bruncevic argues, the characteristics of the hyperobject, which is by definition a complicated and multifaceted construct, map well onto a discussion of art in the context of law and the commons. I will highlight only a few of these characteristics, which, I would suggest, also apply very well to the concept of the posthumanist agential assemblages through which the critical AI art projects I have discussed throughout this book are instantiated.

In particular, Morton's hyperobject is viscous (it has a tendency to spread and cling to material and conceptual contexts beyond itself); nonlocal (it is distributed in time and space, and its nonlocal qualities can outweigh its local manifestations); and interobjective (it connects to a multiplicity of other objects and concepts, and its existence or significance may reveal itself most powerfully in these entanglements). Following this framework, Bruncevic classifies art itself as a hyperobject,[2] and as Morton and a host of collaborators (Morton et al. 2018) have shown, this view can also be extended to creativity more generally. But what about AI art more specifically? In chapter 2, I described as artificially intelligent any assemblages of technologies, operations, functions, and effects that can be meaningfully perceived as resulting from intelligent (or creative) behavior, or which can be identified in outputs that are the results of such behavior. As I have argued, in digital art projects that align with such a definition and which approach AI tactically, both intelligence and creativity can become decoupled from the human, and the centrality of human agency is challenged when it comes to humanist and anthropocentric notions of authorship,

2 Bruncevic's discussion of art in relation to Morton's concept of the hyperobject is considerably more extensive, and extends to all five of the core characteristics Morton describes; see, in particular, Part 2 of her book.

as well as the assimilation of art into complex socio-economic and political systems. All of this, it seems to me, is captured well when AI art itself is considered as a hyperobject. The designation also clarifies that the kinds of critical AI art I have discussed cannot easily be contained by a traditionally conceived cultural commons, nor by the anthropocentric, humanist property enclosures to which such a commons is linked. In critical works of AI art and the posthumanist agential assemblages that produce them, the viscosity, nonlocalness, and interobjectivity of Morton's hyperobject feed directly into the posthumanist cultural commons itself.

This perspective helps overcome what I see as an important problem harbored in the concept of the commons. Traditionally, that which is contained in the commons also facilitates constant threats to the continued existence of the commons, since everything in the resource pool is by definition subject to appropriation into private property enclosures. But the posthumanist cultural commons as I envision it functions differently: here, that which constitutes the commons instead can undermine the possibility of its own removal from the commons. Take, for example, an AI-generated artwork that eludes copyright because it cannot technically be recognized as an authored expression. Its uncertain legal status is arguably determined not merely by some static quality encapsulated in a presumptively authorless aesthetic artefact, but very importantly also by the operational logic of the agential assemblage that produced this artefact. GAN-style AI art, as I have described it earlier in this chapter, is a case in point. It speculatively contradicts the property enclosures to which aesthetic expressions are conventionally subjected, and it does so not because it was created by a machine, but, more importantly, because both the assemblage that created it and the workings of this assemblage elude the traditional definitions of creativity on which IP enclosures conventionally hinge.

Thus, the two key requirements for my posthumanist cultural commons—persistence beyond assumptions of the centrality of human agency, and sustained resistance to assimilation into anthropocentric IP enclosures—are satisfied both in GAN-style AI artworks and in the agential assemblage that will have produced them. The non-human is no longer only object, but also subject of the commons. Or, more specifically: the posthumanist cultural commons is co-constituted both by the works of the posthumanist agential assemblage (certain types of AI art, AI expressions, or, simply, AI outputs) and by its workings (its functionality, operational logic, or perceived behaviors).

This suggestion should not be misinterpreted as technologically deterministic. As I hope to have shown throughout, in its critical figurations the posthumanist agential assemblage does not operate "by design," simply enacting algorithmic routines that execute predetermined protocols. Instead, such an assemblage can continually afford all of its constituent parts all kinds of actions and interventions, and these, in turn, co-determine its functionality, behaviors, outputs, meaning, as well as its very existence. Because these characteristics are inevitably conferred on the posthumanist cultural commons itself, the workings of the posthumanist agential assemblage can also be described as a posthumanist commoning.

Commoning is generally understood as the process of maintaining or reclaiming a commons (Linebaugh 2007). But while this understanding usefully identifies an intimate connection between commons and commoner, it also conveys the notion, well established in political economy and economic theory, that the commons is a resource to be managed (see, for example, Hardin 1968; Ostrom 1990). Conceptualized as a posthumanist ecology, however, the commons no longer relies so fundamentally on resource management through those who are also entitled to exploit it. Instead, when the posthumanist agential assemblage, as hyperobject, disturbs the integrity and perpetuation of IP enclosures, or when it resists assimilation into them, it is itself engaged in a posthumanist process of commoning.

AI, without doubt, manifests in many forms that can amplify the property-oriented logic of capital. My key question, throughout this book, has been what radical interventions AI might nevertheless also be able to stage in this logic. In the figuration of the posthumanist agential assemblage, what sort of a political agent can AI constitute? How is the becoming-agential of AI entangled with human agency? How does the posthumanist agential assemblage figure into existing AI systems that criss-cross capital, surveillance, and new forms of algorithmic governmentality? And how, by contrast, can a critical art of AI feed into tactical opposition to such regimes? The feminist and anarchist scholar Silvia Frederici (2012) writes that commoners can (re)produce themselves as the subjects of the commons. This is precisely what I mean when I think of the "becoming-tactical" of AI: the contribution of artificial intelligence to a larger critical posthumanist project is that it can facilitate a tactical commoning to structurally undermine anthropocentric property enclosures. The commons has become entangled in the struggle of commoning.

The emergence of the posthumanist assemblage in which the agency for expression, creativity, or authorship might be distributed across multiple entities (human and non-human alike) hinges on a radical rethinking of what property means and how it operates, what we mean by cultural ownership, by creativity, by calling something a creative expression. As I have argued, interfaces between technology, culture, and law are important sites of conflict, resistance, and speculative exploration in this regard, since it is here that different domains of human (and non-human) expression are folded into broader socio-economic systems. Artistic experiments with AI are already pushing and reconfiguring the boundaries I've outlined in the preceding chapters. It is through experiments such as Adam Basanta's *All We'd Ever Need Is One Another* or Maja Smrekar's *!brute_force* that it becomes possible to imagine how anthropocentric property relations, in the ways in which they currently manifest in aesthetic artefacts and our dealings with them, may be transcended. In my mind, a core marker of posthumanist art is, in this sense, the emergence of aesthetic hyperobjects that afford defiance of anthropocentric ownership models in all their permutations.

Earlier, I have described the effects of the posthumanist agential assemblage as the production, against the logic of human author- and ownership, of a kind of unownability that manifests in the works and workings of tactical AI. In this spirit, I end my speculative exploration of AI art's critical potential with a question: is posthumanist expressive agency a fundamentally post-ownership concept?

References

Amel Chamandy / Galerie NuEdge Fine Arts v. Adam Basanta [Ongoing] 500-17-104564-185 Quebec Superior Court.

Andersen, Christian U., and Geoff Cox, eds. 2019. *A Peer-Reviewed Journal About* 8 (1) (special issue: "Machine Feeling").

ArtBreeder. n. d. Accessed November 6, 2020. https://www.artbreeder.com/.

"Art Data." n. d. *Artnome.com*. Accessed November 13, 2020. https://www.artnome.com/art-data.

Artnome. 2018. Post on *Twitter.com* from October 26, 2018. Accessed February 15, 2021. https://twitter.com/artnome/status/1055811701445197825.

Asay, Clark. 2020. "Independent Creation in a World of AI." *FIU Law Review* 14 (2): 201–22. https://dx.doi.org/10.25148/lawrev.14.2.5.

Ascari, Maurizio. 2014. "The Dangers of Distant Reading: Reassessing Moretti's Approach to Literary Genres." *Genre* 47 (1): 1–19.

Aufderheide, Patricia, and Peter Jaszi. 2018. *Reclaiming Fair Use: How to Put Balance Back in Copyright*, Second Edition. Chicago: University of Chicago Press.

Bailey, Jason. 2018. "The AI Art At Christie's Is Not What You Think." *Artnome.com*. Accessed November 13, 2020. https://www.artnome.com/news/2018/10/13/the-ai-art-at-christies-is-not-what-you-think.

Barad, Karen. 2007. *Meeting the Universe Halfway: Quantum Physics and the Entanglement of Matter and Meaning*. Durham, NC: Duke University Press.

Barandiaran, Xabier, Ezequiel Di Paolo, and Marieke Rohde. 2009. "Defining Agency: Individuality, Normativity, Asymmetry and Spatio-temporality in Action." *Journal of Adaptive Behavior* 17 (5): 367–86.

Barrat, Robbie. 2018. @videodrome *Twitter* thread. Accessed November 13, 2020. https://twitter.com/videodrome/status/1055285640420483073?lang=en.

———. n. d. Github repository. Accessed November 13, 2020. https://github.com/robbiebarrat.

Bartow, Ann. 2006. "Fair Use and the Fairer Sex: Gender, Feminism, and Copyright Law." *Journal of Gender, Social Policy & the Law* 14 (3): 551–84.

Basanta, Adam. 2018. *All We'd Ever Need Is One Another*. Artwork. Online documentation accessed November 6, 2020. http://allwedeverneed.com/about.html.

Baum, Joan. 1986. *The Calculating Passion of Ada Byron*. Beeston: Shoe String Press.

Bennett, Jane. 2009. *Vibrant Matter: A Political Ecology of Things*. Durham, NC: Duke University Press.

Berkeley Library, University of California. n. d. "Art History: Image Databases." Accessed November 13, 2020. https://guides.lib.berkeley.edu/c.php?g=478634&p=4689064.

Berry, David M. 2019. "Complexities, Explainability and Method: Media Philosophy and Artificial Intelligence." In *Proceedings for DH2019*. Accessed November 13, 2020. https://dev.clariah.nl/files/dh2019/boa/0542.html.

Boden, Margaret. 1990. *The Creative Mind: Myths and Mechanisms*. Milton Park: Routledge.

Boon, Marcus. 2010. *In Praise of Copying*. Cambridge, MA: Harvard University Press.

Borges, Jorge Luis. 1941. "Pierre Menard." In *Labyrinths*, translated by James Irby, 62–71. New York: New Directions.

Boutang, Yann Moulier. 2011. *Cognitive Capitalism*. Cambridge: Polity.

Bown, Oliver. 2015. "Attributing Creative Agency: Are We Doing It Right?" *Proceedings of the Sixth International Conference on Computational Creativity*: 17–22.

Boyle, James. 2008. *Public Domain: Enclosing the Commons of the Mind*. New Haven, CT: Yale University Press.

Braidotti, Rosi. 2013. *The Posthuman*. New York: Polity.

Braidotti, Rosi, and Maria Hlavajova. 2018. *Posthuman Glossary*. London: Bloomsbury.

Bridle, James. 2018. *New Dark Age: Technology and the End of the Future*. London: Verso.

Bridy, Annemarie. 2012. "Coding Creativity: Copyright and the Artificially Intelligent Author." *Stanford Technology Law Review* 5: 1–28.

———. 2016. "The Evolution of Authorship: Work Made by Code." *Columbia Journal of Law & Arts* 39: 395–401.

Bringsjord, Selmer, Paul Bello, and David Ferrucci. 2001. "Creativity, the Turing Test, and the (Better) Lovelace Test." *Minds and Machines* 11: 3–27.

Bruncevic, Merima. 2018. *Law, Art and the Commons*. London: Routledge.

Burk, Dan L. 2019. "Algorithmic Fair Use." *University of Chicago Law Review* 86: 283–307.

Burrell, Gillian. 2019. "Randomly Generated Art Draws Copyright and Trademark Infringement Claims." *IPOsgoode.ca*. Accessed November 13, 2020. https://www.iposgoode.ca/2019/04/.randomly-generated-art-draws-copyright-and-trademark-infringement-claims/.

Butler, Judith. 1998. "Imitation and Gender Insubordination." In *Literary Theory: An Anthology*, edited by Julie Rivkin and Michael Ryan, 722–30. Malden, MA: Blackwell.

CCH Canadian Ltd. v. Law Society of Upper Canada [2004] Supreme Court of Canada 13.

Chamandy, Amel. 2009. *Your World Without Paper*. Artwork.

Chopra, Samir, and Laurence White. 2011. *A Legal Theory for Autonomous Artificial Agents*. Ann Arbor: University of Michigan Press.

Christie's. 2018. "Is Artificial Intelligence Set to Become Art's Next Medium?" *Christies.com*. Accessed November 6, 2020. https://www.christies.com/features/A-collaboration-between-two-artists-one-human-one-a-machine-9332-1.aspx.

Coding Dürer. n. d. "Data Sources." Accessed November 13, 2020. http://codingdurer.de/data.html.

Cole, David. 2020. "The Chinese Room Argument." *The Stanford Encyclopedia of Philosophy* (Spring 2020 Edition), edited by Edward N. Zalta. Accessed November 12, 2020. https://plato.stanford.edu/archives/spr2020/entries/chinese-room/.

Coombe, Rosemary J. 1994. "Challenging Paternity: Histories of Copyright." *Yale Journal of Law and Humanities* 6: 397–422.

———. 1998. *The Cultural Life of Intellectual Property: Authorship, Appropriation, and the Law*. Durham, NC: Duke University Press.

Coombe, Rosemary J., Darren Wershler and Martin Zeilinger, eds. 2014. *Dynamic Fair Dealing: Creating Canadian Culture Online*. Toronto: University of Toronto Press.

Copeland, Jack B. 2020. "The Church-Turing Thesis", *The Stanford Encyclopedia of Philosophy (Summer 2020 Edition)*, edited by Edward N. Zalta. Accessed November 6, 2020. https://plato.stanford.edu/archives/sum2020/entries/church-turing/.

Craig, Carys. 2015. "Feminist Aesthetics and Copyright Law: Genius, Value, and Gendered Visions of the Creative Self." In *Diversity in Intellectual Property: Identities, Interests, and Intersections*, edited by Irene Calboli and Srividhya Ragavan, 273–93. Cambridge: Cambridge University Press.

Craig, Carys, and Ian Kerr. 2021. "The Death of the AI Author." *Ottawa Law Review* 52 (1): 31–86. https://rdo-olr.org/2021/the-death-of-the-ai-author/.

Crawford, Kate, and Trevor Paglen. 2019. *ImageNet Roulette*. Artwork.

———. 2019b. "Excavating AI: The Politics of Images in Machine Learning Training Sets." Accessed November 6, 2020. https://www.excavating.ai/.

Critical Art Ensemble. 2001. *Digital Resistance: Explorations in Tactical Media*. New York: Autonomedia.

Darling, Kate. 2017. "Who's Johnny? Anthropomorphic Framing in Human-Robot Interaction, Integration, and Policy." In *Robot Ethics 2.0: From Autonomous Cars to Artificial Intelligence*, edited by Patrick Lin, Keith Abney and Ryan Jenkins, 173–92. Oxford: Oxford University Press.

Davidson, Donald. 1980. "Actions, Reasons, and Causes," in *Essays on Actions and Events*, 3–20. Oxford: Clarendon Press.

de Certeau, Michel. 2011. *The Practice of Everyday Life*. Berkeley: University of California Press.

Dean, Jodi. 2005. "Communicative Capitalism: Circulation and the Foreclosure of Politics." *Cultural Politics* 1 (1): 51–74.

Deeks, Ashley. 2019. "The Judicial Demand for Explainable Artificial Intelligence." *Columbia Law Review* 119: 1829–50.

Drahos, Peter. 1996. *A Philosophy of Intellectual Property*. Dartmouth: Aldershot.

Dougherty, Stephen. 2001. "Culture in the Disk Drive: Computationalism, Memetics, and the Rise of Posthumanism." *Diacritics* 31 (4): 85–102.

du Sautoy, Marcus. 2019. *The Creativity Code: Art and Innovation in the Age of AI*. Cambridge, MA: Harvard University Press.

Dyer-Witheford, Nick, Atle Mikkola Kjosen, and James Steinhoff. 2019. *Inhuman Power: Artificial Intelligence and the Future of Capitalism*. London: Pluto Press.

Edwards, Dustin W. 2018. "Circulation Gatekeepers: Unbundling the Platform Politics of YouTube's Content ID." *Computers and Composition* 47: 61–74.

Elgammal, Ahmed, Marian Mazzone, Bingchen Liu, Diana Kim, and Mohamed Elhoseiny. 2018. "The Shape of Art History in the Eyes of the Machine." *Proceedings of the 32nd AAAi conference on Artificial Intelligence*: 1–25. arXiv:1801.07729v1.

Elkin-Koren, Niva. 2017. "Copyright in a Digital Ecosystem: A User-Rights Approach." In *Copyright Law in an Age of Limitations and Exceptions*, edited by Ruth L. Ojediji, 132–68. Cambridge: Cambridge University Press.

———. 2019. "Fair Use By Design." *UCLA Law Review* 64: 1082–1100.

Elwes, Jake. 2016. *Machine Learning Porn*. Artwork. Online documentation accessed November 6, 2020. https://www.jakeelwes.com/project-MLPorn.html.

———. 2019. *Zizi*. Artwork. Online documentation accessed November 6, 2020. https://www.jakeelwes.com/project-zizi-2019.html.

———. 2019b. "Machine Learning & Art." *Youtube.com*. Accessed November 13, 2020. https://www.youtube.com/watch?v=4_tLqkXKhE0&vl=en.

———. 2021. *The Zizi Show*. Artwork. Accessed March 20, 2021. https://zizi.ai/.

Elsevier. n. d. "Text and Data Mining." Accessed November 13, 2020. arXiv:1801.07729v1.

Evans, David, ed. 2009. *Appropriation*. Cambridge, MA: MIT Press.

Eve, Paul Martin. 2019. *Close Reading with Computers Textual Scholarship, Computational Formalism, and David Mitchell's Cloud Atlas*. Redwood City, CA: Stanford University Press.

Farr, Evan H. 1989. "Copyrightability of Computer-Created Works." *Rutgers Computer and Technology Law Review* 15: 63.

Feist Publications, Inc v. Rural Telephone Service Co [1991] US Supreme Court 50.

Finn, Ed. 2017. *What Algorithms Want: Imagination in the Age of Computing*. Cambridge, MA: MIT Press.

Flickr-Faces-HQ Dataset (FFHQ) Dataset of Human Faces for Generative Adversarial Networks (GAN). n. d. *Kaggle.com*. Accessed November 13, 2020. https://www.kaggle.com/arnaud58/flickrfaceshq-dataset-ffhq/version/1.

Foucault, Michel. 1980. "What Is an Author?" In *Language, Counter-Memory, Practice: Selected Essays and Interviews by Michel Foucault*, edited by Donald F. Bouchard, 113–38. Ithaca, NY: Cornell University Press.

Frankfurt, Harry. 1971. "Freedom of the Will and the Concept of a Person." *Journal of Philosophy* 68 (1): 5–20.

Frederici, Silvia. 2012. *Revolution at Point Zero Housework, Reproduction, and Feminist Struggle*. Oakland, CA: PM Press.

French, Martin, Adrian Guta, Marilou Gagnon, Eric Mykhalovskiy, Stephen L Roberts, Su Goh, Alexander McClelland and Fenwick McKelvey. 2020. "Corporate contact tracing as a pandemic response." *Critical Public Health*. https://doi.org/10.1080/09581596.2020.1829549.

Galloway, Alexander R. 2004. *Protocol: How Control Exists after Decentralization*. Cambridge, MA: MIT Press.

Gaines, Jane M. 1991. *Contested Culture: The Image, the Voice, and the Law*. Chapel Hill, NC: University of North Carolina Press.

Gillespie, Tarleton. 2016. "Designed to 'Effectively Frustrate': Copyright, Technology and the Agency of Users." *New Media & Society* 8 (4): 651–69.

Goh, Gabriel. n. d. "Image Synthesis from Yahoo's open_nsfw." *Gwern.net*. Accessed November 14, 2020. https://www.gwern.net/docs/ai/2016-goh-opennsfw.html.

Goodfellow, Ian, Jean Pouget-Abadie, Mehdi Mirza, Bing Xu, David Warde-Farley, Sherjil Ozair, Aaron Courville, Yoshua Bengio. 2014. "Generative Adversarial Networks." Accessed November 13, 2020. arXiv:1406.2661.

Grier, David A. 2005. *When Computers Were Human*. Princeton, NJ: Princeton University Press.

Grimmelmann, James. 2016. "There's No Such Thing as a Computer-Authored Work—and It's a Good Thing, Too." *Columbia Journal of Law & Arts* 39 (3): 403-16.

Guihot, Michael, and Matthew Rimmer. 2019. "Artificial Intelligence: Governance and Leadership—A Submission to the Australian Human Rights Commission and World Economic Forum." *Australian Human Rights Commission and World Economic Forum*. Accessed November 6, 2020. https://eprints.qut.edu.au/127442/.

Gunkel, David J. 2017. "Special Section: Rethinking Art and Aesthetics in the Age of Creative Machines." *Philosophy & Technology* 30 (3): 1–3.

Guo, Yandong, Lei Zhang, Yuxiao Hu, Xiaodong He, and Jianfeng Gao. 2016. "MS-Celeb-1M: A Dataset and Benchmark for Large-Scale Face Recognition." In *Computer Vision—Proceedings of ECCV 2016*: 87-102. https://doi.org/10.1007/978-3-319-46487-9_6.

Halbert, Deborah. 2005. *Resisting Intellectual Property*. Milton Park: Routledge.

Hall, Gary. 2016. *Pirate Philosophy: For a Digital Posthumanities*. Cambridge, MA: MIT Press.

Hannay, Chris. 2018. "Artist Faces Lawsuit over Computer System that Creates Randomly Generated Images." *TheGlobeandMail.com*. Accessed November 13, 2020. https://www.theglobeandmail.com/arts/art-and-architecture/article-artist-faces-lawsuit-over-computer-system-that-creates-randomly/.

Hardin, Garrett. 1968. "The Tragedy of the Commons." *Science* 162: 1243–48. https://doi.org/10.1126/science.162.3859.1243.

Hardt, Michael, and Antonio Negri. 2009. *Commonwealth*. Cambridge, MA: Harvard University Press.

Hattenbach, Ben, and Joshua Glucoft. 2015. "Patents in an Era of Infinite Monkeys and Artificial Intelligence." *Stanford Technology Law Review* 19: 32–51.

Hayles, Katherine N. 1999. *How We Became Posthuman: Virtual Bodies in Cybernetics, Literature, and Informatics*. Chicago: University of Chicago Press.

———. 2005. *My Mother Was a Computer: Digital Subjects and Literary Texts*. Chicago: University of Chicago Press.

Hegel, G. W. F. 1952. *The Philosophy of Right*. Translated by T. M. Knox. Oxford: Clarendon Press.

Heldt, Amelie Pia. 2019. "Upload-Filters: Bypassing Classical Concepts of Censorship?" *Journal of Intellectual Property, Information Technology and Electronic Commerce Law* 10 (1): 57–65.

Hemment, Drew. 2019. "Preternatural: An Exhibition of Works by Jake Elwes." *Edinburgh Futures Institute*. Accessed November 13, 2020. https://efi.ed.ac.uk/wp-content/uploads/2019/09/Preternatural_Curatorial_Statement_2_August_2019.pdf.

Hertzmann, Aaron. 2018. "Can Computers Create Art?" *Arts* 7 (2): 18–25.

Hesmondalgh, David. 2012. *The Creative Industries*. Third Edition. Newbury Park, CA: Sage Publications.

Hristov, Kalin. 2017. "Artificial Intelligence and the Copyright Dilemma." IDEA 57 (3): 431–54.

Hughes, Justin. 1988. "The Philosophy of Intellectual Property." *Georgetown Law Journal* 77: 289–365.

Hyde, Lewis. 2010. *Common as Air.* New York: Farrar, Straus & Giroux.
Infopaq International A/A v. Danske Dagblades Forening [2009] European Court of Justice 17.
ImageNet. 2016. Accessed November 12, 2020. http://www.image-net.org/.
———. 2016b. "Download FAQ." Accessed November 12, 2020. Archived at https://web.archive.org/web/20201112034227/http://image-net.org/download-faq.
Impett, Leonardo. 2017. "Ways of Machine Seeing." *CRASSH.cam.ac.uk.* Accessed November 12, 2020. http://www.crassh.cam.ac.uk/blog/post/ways-of-machine-seeing.
Jaszi, Peter. 1991. "Toward a Theory of Copyright: The Metamorphoses of 'Authorship'." *Duke Law Journal*: 455–502. Accessed November 14, 2020. https://scholarship.law.duke.edu/dlj/vol40/iss2/8.
Jiang, Jialei. 2019. "What Monkeys Teach Us About Authorship: Toward a Distributed Agency in Digital Composing Practices." *Kairos: A Journal of Rhetoric, Technology, and Pedagogy* 24 (1): n. p. Accessed November 12, 2020. http://kairos.technorhetoric.net/24.1/topoi/jiang/index.html.
Kurzweil, Ray. 2005. *The Singularity Is Near: When Humans Transcend Biology.* New York: Viking.
Land, Nick. 2012. *Fanged Noumena: Collected Writings 1987–2007.* Falmouth: Urbanomic.
Latour, Bruno. 1996. "On Actor-Network Theory: A Few Clarifications." *Soziale Welt* 47 (4): 369–81.
Lessig, Lawrence. 2004. *Free Culture.* London: Penguin.
Levine, Sherrie. 1981. *After Walker Evans.* Artwork.
Linebaugh, Peter. 2007. *Magna Carta Manifesto: Liberties and Commons for All.* Berkeley: University of California Press.
Locke, John. 1690. *Two Treatises of Government, Book II.* Accessed November 14, 2020. https://www.johnlocke.net/major-works/two-treatises-of-government-book-ii.
"Machine Learning Porn." n. d. *Reddit.com.* Accessed November 14, 2020. https://www.reddit.com/r/MLporn/.
Manovich, Lev. 2019. "Defining AI Arts: Three Proposals." *Manovich.net.* Accessed November 6, 2020. http://manovich.net/index.php/projects/defining-ai-arts-three-proposals.
———. 2020. *Cultural Analytics.* Cambridge, MA: MIT Press.
Markoff, John. 2015. *Machines of Loving Grace: The Quest for Common Ground Between Humans and Robots.* New York: Ecco.
Mazzone, Marian, and Ahmed Elgammal. 2019. "Art, Creativity, and the Potential of Artificial Intelligence." *Arts* 8 (1): 1–9. https://doi.org/10.3390/arts8010026.
McClean, Daniel, and Karsten Schubert. 2002. *Dear Images: Art, Copyright and Culture.* London: Ridinghouse.
McCorduck, Pamela. 2004. *Machines Who Think.* Natick, MA: A. K. Peters.
McLeod, Kembrew. 2007. *Owning Culture: Authorship, Ownership, and Intellectual Property Law.* Frankfurt: Peter Lang.
Miller, Arthur I. 2019. *The Artist in the Machine: The World of AI-Powered Creativity.* Cambridge, MA: MIT Press.

Mizrahi, Sarit K. 2019. "Jack of All Trades, Master of None: Is Copyright Protection Justified for Robotic Faux-Riginality?" In *Proceedings for WeRobot 2019*, 1–26. https://robots.law.miami.edu/2019/wp-content/uploads/2019/03/SaritKMizrahi_WeRobot_Article.pdf.

Moretti, Franco. 2000. "Conjectures on World Literature." *New Left Review* 1: 54–68.

Morrison, Wayne, ed. 2001. *Blackstone's Commentaries on the Laws of England (4 Volumes)*. London: Routledge.

Morton, Timothy. 2013. *Hyperobjects: Philosophy and Ecology after the End of the World*. Minneapolis: University of Minnesota Press.

Morton, Timothy, Laura Copelin, and Peyton Gardner, eds. 2018. *Hyperobjects for Artists*. Marfa, TX: Ballroom Marfa and The Creative Independent. Accessed November 14, 2020. https://thecreativeindependent.com/library/hyperobjects-for-artists/.

Murgia, Madhumita. 2019a. "Who's Using Your Face? The Ugly Truth about Facial Recognition." *FT.com*. Accessed November 13, 2020. https://www.ft.com/content/cf19b956-60a2-11e9-b285-3acd5d43599e.

———. 2019b. "Microsoft Quietly Deletes Largest Public Face Recognition Data Set." *FT.com*. Accessed November 13, 2020. https://www.ft.com/content/7d3e0d6a-87a0-11e9-a028-86cea8523dc2.

Naffine, Ngaire. 2003. "Who Are Law's Persons? From Cheshire Cats to Responsible Subjects." *Modern Law Review* 66 (3): 346–67.

Naruto, et al. v. Slater, et al. 2018. No. 16-15469 (9th Cir.) Court opinion. Accessed November 12, 2020. http://cdn.ca9.uscourts.gov/datastore/opinions/2018/04/23/16-15469.pdf.

Nedelsky, Jennifer. 2011. *Law's Relations: A Relational Theory of Self, Autonomy, and Law*. New York, NY: Oxford University Press.

Nguyen, Anh, Alexey Dosovitskiy, Jason Yosinski, Thomas Brox, and Jeff Clune. 2016. "Synthesizing the preferred inputs for neurons in neural networks via deep generator networks." In *Proceedings of the 29th Conference on Neural Information Processing Systems (NIPS)*. arXiv:submit/1578762.

Noll, Michael A. 1963. *Gaussian Quadratic*. Artwork.

———. 1994. "Beginnings of Computer Art." *Leonardo* 27 (1): 39–44.

O'Neill, Eddie. 2019. "API Updates and Important Changes." *Facebook.com*. Accessed November 12, 2020. https://developers.facebook.com/blog/post/2019/04/25/api-updates/.

Obvious Collective. 2018. *Portrait of Edmond Belamy*. Artwork.

Oliver, Julian, Gordan Savičić, and Danja Vasiliev. n. d. "The Critical Engineering Manifesto." Accessed November 12, 2020. https://zkm.de/en/the-critical-engineering-manifesto.

open_nsfw. n. d. *Github.com*. Accessed November 13, 2020. https://github.com/yahoo/open_nsfw.

Ostrom, Elinor. 1990. *Governing the Commons: The Evolution of Institutions for Collective Action*. Cambridge: Cambridge University Press.

Palmer, Tom G. 2005. "Are Patents and Copyrights Morally Justified?" In *Information Ethics. Privacy, Property, and Power*, edited by Adam D. Moore, 123–68. Seattle: University of Washington Press.

Parliament of Great Britain. 1710. *Statute of Anne (Copyright Act of 1710)*. Accessed November 14, 2020. http://www.copyrighthistory.com/anne.html.

Pasquale, Frank. 2015. *The Black Box Society: The Secret Algorithms That Control Money and Information*. Cambridge, MA: Harvard University.

———. 2019. "A Rule of Persons, Not Machines: The Limits of Legal Automation." *George Washington Law Review* 87 (1): 1–56.

Pasquinelli, Matteo. 2019. "How a Machine Learns and Fails—A Grammar of Error for Artificial Intelligence." *Spheres—Journal for Digital Cultures* 5: 1–17. https://spheres-journal.org/wp-content/uploads/spheres-5_Pasquinelli.pdf.

Patry, William. 2005. "Independent Creation: A Bulwark of Copyright." Accessed November 13, 2020. http://williampatry.blogspot.com/2005/06/independent-creation-bulwark-of.html.

Paul, Christiane, ed. 2016. *A Companion to Digital Art*. Hoboken, NJ: Wiley & Sons.

Pepi, Mike. 2018. "Could There Ever Be an AI Artist?" *frieze*. Accessed February 4, 2021. https://www.frieze.com/article/could-there-ever-be-ai-artist.

Pisters, Patricia. 2018. "Body Without Organs." In *Posthuman Glossary*, edited by Rosi Braidotti and Maria Hlavajova, 74–76. London: Bloomsbury.

Public Relations Consultants Association Ltd v. The Newspaper Licensing Agency Ltd [2013] UK Supreme Court 18.

Lessig, Lawrence 2004. *Free Culture: How Big Media Uses Technology and the Law to Lock Down Culture and Control Creativity*. New York: Penguin Random House.

Radin, Margaret. 1982. "Property and Personhood." *Stanford Law Review* 34 (5): 957–1016.

———. 1993. *Reinterpreting Property*. Chicago: University of Chicago Press.

Ramalho, Ana. 2017. "Will Robots Rule the (Artistic) World? a Proposed Model for the Legal Status of Creations by Artificial Intelligence Systems." Accessed November 6, 2020. https://doi.org/10.2139/ssrn.2987757.

Re, Richard M. and Alicia Solow-Niederman. 2019. "Developing Artificially Intelligent Justice." *Stanford Technology Law Review* 22: 242-289.

Rea, Naomi. 2019. "How ImageNet Roulette, an Art Project That Went Viral by Exposing Facial Recognition's Biases, Is Changing People's Minds About AI." *Artnet.com*. Accessed November 12, 2020. https://news.artnet.com/art-world/imagenet-roulette-trevor-paglen-kate-crawford-1658305.

Ridler, Anna. 2019. *Mosaic Virus*. Artwork. Online documentation accessed November 6, 2020. http://annaridler.com/mosaic-virus.

———. 2020. "The Abstraction of Nature." Artist talk at Aksioma (Lljubljana). Accessed November 6, 2020. https://vimeo.com/396388790.

Riley, Rita. 2009. *Tactical Media*. Minneapolis: University of Minnesota Press.

Rose, Mark. 1995. *Authors and Owners: The Invention of Copyright*. Cambridge, MA: Harvard University Press.

Russell, Stuart, and Peter Norvig. 2009. *Artificial Intelligence: A Modern Approach*. 3rd edition. Saddle River, NJ: Prentice Hall.

Saint-Amour, Paul K. 2003. *The Copywrights: Intellectual Property and the Literary Imagination*. Ithaca, NY: Cornell University Press.

Sag, Matthew. 2009. "Copyright and Copy-Reliant Technologies." *Northwestern University Law Review* 103 (4): 1607–82.

———. 2017. "Internet Safe Harbors and the Transformation of Copyright Law." *Notre Dame Law Review* 93 (2): 499–564.

———. 2019. "The New Legal Landscape for Text Mining and Machine Learning." *Journal of the Copyright Society of the USA* 66 (2): 291–340.

Saltz, Jerry. 2018. "An Artwork Made by Artificial Intelligence Just Sold for $400,000. I Am Shocked, Confused, Appalled." *Vulture*. Accessed February 4, 2021. https://www.vulture.com/2018/10/an-artificial-intelligence-artwork-just-sold-for-usd400-000.html.

Samuelson, Pamela. 1985. "Allocating Ownership Rights in Computer-Generated Works." *University of Pittsburgh Law Review* 47: 1185–1228.

Sarin, Helena. 2018. "Playing a game of GANstruction." *The Gradient*. Accessed October 14, 2020. https://thegradient.pub/playing-a-game-of-ganstruction/.

Scarlett, Ashley. 2020. "Artist Residency Programming & the Early Histories of Computer Graphics Research in Canada." In *Computational Arts in Canada 1967–1974*, edited by Adam Lauder, 57–78. London, ON: McIntosh Gallery.

Scassa, Teresa. 2018. "Artist sued in Canada for copyright infringement for AI-related art project." Accessed November 13, 2020. http://www.teresascassa.ca/index.php?option=com_k2&view=item&id=286:artist-sued-in-canada-for-copyright-infringement-for-ai-related-art-project.

Schnably, Stephen. 1993. "Property and Pragmatism: A Critique of Radin's Theory of Property and Personhood." *Stanford Law Review* 45: 347–407.

Schlosser, Markus. 2019. "Agency." *The Stanford Encyclopedia of Philosophy* (Winter 2019 Edition), edited by Edward N. Zalta. Accessed November 12, 2020. https://plato.stanford.edu/archives/win2019/entries/agency/.

Schroeder, Jeanne L. 2006. "Unnatural Rights: Hegel and Intellectual Property." *University of Miami Law Review* 60 (4): 453–504.

Scott, James. 1998. *Seeing Like a State: How Certain Schemes to Improve the Human Condition Have Failed*. New Haven, CT: Yale University Press.

Shaw, Anny. 2018. "Who Needs Artists? Rise in Works Made by Artificial Intelligence Raises Real Questions for the Art Market" *The Art Newspaper*. Accessed February 4, 2021. https://www.theartnewspaper.com/analysis/rise-in-works-made-by-artificial-intelligence-raises-real-questions.

Sheldon v. Metro-Goldwyn Pictures Corporation, 81 F.2d 49 (2d Cir. 1936). Accessed February 5, 2021. https://law.justia.com/cases/federal/appellate-courts/F2/81/49/1475281/.

Searle, John. 1980. "Minds, Brains and Programs." *Behavioral and Brain Sciences* 3: 417–57.

Sedgewick, Robert, and Kevin Wayne. 2011. *Algorithms*. Fourth Edition. Boston, MA.: Pearson Education.

Smrekar, Maja. Ongoing. *!brute_force*. Artwork. Online documentation accessed November 6, 2020. https://www.nonbruteforce.net/.

———. 2020. "!brute_force." Video, commissioned by the Ars Electronica AI Lab.

———. n. d. "!brute_force." Accessed November 14, 2020. https://www.majasmrekar.org/brute_force.

———. n. d. "What Can Artificial Intelligence Learn From Dogs?" Accessed November 14, 2020. https://www.nonbruteforce.net/research1.

———. n. d. "Canine Data Training." Accessed November 14, 2020. https://www.nonbruteforce.net/research2.

———. n. d. "Towards the Final Concept Frame." Accessed November 14, 2020. https://www.nonbruteforce.net/research4.

Snell, Ben. 2020. Post on *Instagram.com*. Accessed November 6, 2020. https://www.instagram.com/p/B8bT6kSlvHs/.

———. n. d. *Contrapposto*. Artwork (online documentation). Accessed November 6, 2020. http://bensnell.io/inheritance-ii.

Solum, Lawrence B. 1992. "Legal Personhood for Artificial Intelligences." *North Carolina Law Review* 70: 1231–87.

Steinert, Steffen. 2017. "Art: Brought to You by Creative Machines." *Philosophy & Technology* 30 (3): 267–84.

Sternberg, Robert J., ed. 2011. *Handbook of Creativity*. Cambridge: Cambridge University Press.

Stiegler, Bernard. 1998. *Technics and Time*, Volume 1. Redwood City, CA: Stanford University Press.

———. 2019. *The Age of Disruption: Technology and Madness in Computational Capitalism*. New York: Polity Press.

Sunder, Madhavi. 1996. "Authorship and Autonomy as Rites of Exclusion: the Intellectual Propertization of Free Speech in *Hurley v. Irish-American Gay, Lesbian, and Bisexual Group of Boston*." *Stanford Law Review* 49 (1): 143–72. https://doi.org/10.2307/1229374.

Taylor, Charles. 1977. "What Is Human Agency?" In *The Self: Psychological and Philosophical Issues*, edited by Theodore Mischel, 103–135. Oxford: Blackwell.

Taylor, Grant. 2014. *When the Machine Made Art: The Troubled History of Computer Art*. London: Bloomsbury.

Tehranian, John. 2015. "The New ©ensorship." *Iowa Law Review* 101. https://ilr.law.uiowa.edu/print/volume-101-issue-1/the-new-censorship/.

Thompson, Jeff. 2020. *Human Computers*. Artwork. Online documentation accessed November 14, 2020. http://www.jeffreythompson.org/human-computers.php.

Titlow, John P. 2016. "How YouTube Is Fixing Its Most Controversial Feature." *Fastcompany.com*. Accessed November 13, 2020. https://www.fastcompany.com/3062494/how-youtube-is-fixing-its-most-controversial-feature.

Transmediale. n.d. "Adversarial Hacking in the Age of AI: Call for Proposals." Accessed November 12, 2020. https://2020.transmediale.de/content/adversarial-hacking-in-the-age-of-ai-call-for-proposals.

Tufekci, Zeynep. 2015. "Algorithmic Harms Beyond Facebook and Google: Emergent Challenges of Computational Agency." *Journal on Telecommunications and High Technology Law* 13: 203–18.

Turing, Alan. 1950. "Computing Machinery and Intelligence." *Mind* 59 (236): 433–60.

UK Copyright and Rights in Performances Regulations 2014, section 29A. Accessed November 13, 2020. http://www.legislation.gov.uk/uksi/2014/1372/regulation/3/made.

UK Copyright, Designs and Patents Act 1988. Accessed November 12, 2020. https://www.legislation.gov.uk/ukpga/1988/48/contents.

U.S. Copyright Office. 2017. *Compendium of U.S. Copyright Office Practices § 101* (Third Edition). Accessed November 12, 2020. https://www.copyright.gov/comp3/.

Vaidhyanathan, Siva. 2001. *Copyrights and Copywrongs: The Rise of Intellectual Property and how it Threatens Creativity*. New York: New York University Press.

van den Hoven van Genderen, Robert. 2018. "Do We Need New Legal Personhood in the Age of Robots and AI?" In *Robotics, AI and the Future of Law. Perspectives in Law, Business and Innovation*, edited by M. Corrales, M. Fenwick and N. Forgó, 15–55. Singapore: Springer Singapore. https://doi.org/10.1007/978-981-13-2874-9_2.

Vaver, David. 2006. "Intellectual Property: The State of the Art." In *Intellectual Property Rights: Critical Concepts in Law*, edited by David Vaver. London: Routledge.

Vincent, James. 2016. "This AI Program Sees Genitals Everywhere It Looks ." *TheVerge.com*. Accessed November 13, 2020. https://www.theverge.com/2016/10/24/13379208/ai-nsfw-neural-nets-deep-dream-genitals.

———. 2018. "How Three French Students Used Borrowed Code To Put the First AI Portrait in Christie's." *TheVerge.com*. Accessed November 13, 2020. https://www.theverge.com/2018/10/23/18013190/ai-art-portrait-auction-christies-belamy-obvious-robbie-barrat-gans.

———. 2019. "This AI-generated Sculpture Is Made from the Shredded Remains of the Computer that Designed it." *TheVerge.com*. Accessed November 6, 2020. https://www.theverge.com/tldr/2019/4/12/18306090/ai-generated-sculpture-shredded-remains-ben-snell-dio.

Wark, McKenzie. 2004. *A Hacker Manifesto*. Cambridge, MA: Harvard University Press.

White, Tom. n.d. "portrait-gan." Software repository on *Github.com*. Accessed February 15, 2021. https://github.com/dribnet/portrain-gan.

Wirtén, Eva Hemmungs. 2004. *No Trespassing: Authorship, Intellectual Property Rights, and the Boundaries of Globalization*. Toronto: University of Toronto Press.

Wojcicki, Susan. 2017. "Expanding Our Work against Abuse of Our Platform." *Youtube.com*. Accessed November 13, 2020. https://blog.youtube/news-and-events/expanding-our-work-against-abuse-of-our.

Wong, Julie C. 2019. "The Viral Selfie App ImageNet Roulette Seemed Fun—Until It Called Me a Racist Slur." *Theguardian.com*. Accessed November 12, 2020. https://www.theguardian.com/technology/2019/sep/17/imagenet-roulette-asian-racist-slur-selfie.

Wu, Tim. 2019. "Will Artificial Intelligence Eat the Law? The Rise of Hybrid Social-Ordering Systems." *Columbia Law Review* 119: 2001–28.

Yamamoto, Takashi B. 2018. "AI Created Works and Copyright." *Patents Licensing* 48 (1): 1–16.

Yanisky-Ravid, Shlomit, and Luis A. Velez-Hernandez. 2018. "Copyrightability of Artworks Produced by Creative Robots and Originality: The Formality-Objective Model." *Minnesota Journal of Law, Science and Technology* 19 (1): 1–53.

Yang, Kaiyu, Qinami, Klint, Fei-Fei, Li, Deng, Jia, and Olga Russakovsky. 2019. "Towards Fairer Datasets: Filtering and Balancing the Distribution of the People Subtree in the ImageNet Hierarchy." Accessed November 12, 2020. http://image-net.org/update-sep-17-2019.php.

YouTube. n. d. "Using Content ID." Accessed November 13, 2020. https://support.google.com/youtube/answer/3244015.

Yu, Robert. 2017. "The Machine Author: What Level of Copyright Protection Is Appropriate for Fully Independent Computer-Generated Works?" *University of Pennsylvania Law Review* 165: 1245–70.

Yuan, Raymond. 2018. "Neural Style Transfer: Creating Art with Deep Learning Using tf.keras and Eager Execution." *Medium.com* Accessed November 6, 2020. https://medium.com/tensorflow/neural-style-transfer-creating-art-with-deep-learning-using-tf-keras-and-eager-execution-7d541ac31398.

Zeilinger, Martin. 2009. *Art and Politics of Appropriation*. Unpublished PhD Thesis, Toronto: University of Toronto.

———. 2012. "Chiptuning Intellectual Property: Digital Culture Between Creative Commons and Moral Economy." *Journal of the International Association for the Study of Popular Music*. 3 (1): 19–34.

———. 2017. "Métic Action in Digital Culture." *Platform Journal* 8 (1): 8–23.

———. 2021. "Generative Adversarial Copy Machines." *Culture Machine* 20 (special issue, "Machine Intelligences in Context: Beyond the Technological Sublime," guest-edited by Peter Jakobsson, Anne Kaun & Fredrik Stiernstedt).

Zuboff, Shoshana. 2019. *The Age of Surveillance Capitalism: The Fight for a Human Future at the New Frontier of Power*. London: Profile Books.

Zygmunt, Justyna. 2016. "To Teach a Machine a Sense of Art—Problems with Automated Methods of Fighting Copyright Infringements on the Example of YouTube Content ID." *Proceedings of Machine Ethics and Machine Law Conference*, Jagiellonian University: 55–56.

Zylinska, Joanna. 2020. *AI Art: Machine Visions and Warped Dreams*. London: Open Humanities Press.

www.ingramcontent.com/pod-product-compliance
Ingram Content Group UK Ltd.
Pitfield, Milton Keynes, MK11 3LW, UK
UKHW041951190726
13854UKWH00005B/1911